UNITED STATE ATLAS ROAD MAP (Full-Colour Travel Guide 2025-2026)

Explore America's National Geographical Iconic Adventures, Must-See Parks Destinations , through Calender and Expert Travel Insights

Goldenpath journeyman Guide

distribute it by any other pars without the consent of the writer

Table of Contents

INTRODUCTION

CHAPTER 1: Welcome to the Ultimate Road to atlas

CHAPTER 2: How to Use This Guidebook

CHAPTER 3: Why Explore the U.S. by Road in 2025-2026

CHAPTER 4: Essential Packing Tips for Road Travelers

CHAPTER 5: Staying Safe and Healthy on the Road

CHAPTER 6: Planning Your Journey

Road Trip Planning Basics

Choosing Your Route

Budgeting for Your Trip

Weather Considerations by Region

CHAPTER 7: Navigating the United States

Understanding the Atlas Maps

Key Symbols and Features of This Guide

Driving Laws and Rules by State

CHAPTER 8: Transportation Options

Renting Cars, RVs, or Campervans

Tips for Electric Vehicle (EV) Travelers

Using Public Transit and Rideshares

Regional Highlights and Scenic Routes

CHAPTER 9: Northeast

Must-See Attractions (e.g., Acadia National Park, NYC Landmarks)

Best Scenic Drives (e.g., Kancamagus Highway, Hudson Valley)

Seasonal Highlights (Fall Foliage, Winter Skiing)

CHAPTER 10: South

Historic Routes (e.g., Civil Rights Trail, Natchez Trace Parkway)

Coastal Escapes (e.g., Florida Keys, Outer Banks)

Foodie Road Trips (e.g., BBQ Trails, Bourbon Country)

CHAPTER 11: Midwest
Classic Drives (e.g., Route 66, Great River Road)

Lakeside Adventures (e.g., Great Lakes Shores, Mackinac Island)

Rural Gems and State Fairs

CAPTER 12: West

Iconic Drives (e.g., Pacific Coast Highway, Going-to-the-Sun Road)

National Parks (e.g., Yellowstone, Yosemite, Grand Canyon)

Wine Country Routes (California, Oregon)

Accommodations and Dining

CAPTER13: Finding the Perfect Place to Stay

Hotels, Motels, and Inns

Best Campgrounds and RV Parks

Unique Stays (e.g., Glamping, Historic Lodges)

CAPTER 14: Where to Eat on the Road

Roadside Diners and Food Trucks

Regional Specialties by State

Budget-Friendly Dining Options

Activities and Entertainment

CAPTER 15: Outdoor Adventures

Hiking, Biking, and Kayaking Trails

Beaches and Waterfront Getaways

Wildlife Watching and National Park Activities

CAPTER16: Nightlife and Entertainment

Live Music Venues

Bars and Clubs by City

Unique Nighttime Activities (e.g., Stargazing Spots)

CHAPTER 17: Shopping and Souvenirs

Best Places for Local Crafts and Artisan Goods

Outlet Malls and Antique Shops

Practical Tips and Resources

CAPTER 18: Road Trip Survival Guide

Dealing with Emergencies

Apps and Gadgets for Travelers

Tips for Traveling with Kids and Pets

CAPTER 19: Budget Travel Tips

Saving on Fuel, Accommodations, and Food

Free and Low-Cost Attractions

Discounts for Seniors, Veterans, and Students

CHAPTER 20: Laws and Safety Tips

State-Specific Driving Laws

Rules for National and State Parks

Important Emergency Numbers

Extras and Appendices

21:. Directory of U.S. Traval

State Tourism Offices

Emergency Contacts

Useful Websites and Apps

22. Index of Maps and Destinations

23 Acknowledgments

How Cynthia Toured the United States on a Budget Using the United States Atlas Road Map Travel Guide

Cynthia had always dreamed of exploring the United States, but as a recent college graduate with student loans and a modest savings account, her wanderlust seemed impossible to satisfy. Then, while browsing her local bookstore, she stumbled upon the United States Atlas Road Map Travel Guide 2025-2026. The colorful cover promised "affordable adventures," and flipping through the pages, Cynthia realized this might be the key to making her dream trip a reality.

The Spark of Adventure

Armed with her new guidebook, Cynthia spent a weekend planning her trip. The guide's budget travel section caught her eye immediately. It laid out practical tips on saving money on accommodations, dining, and attractions. The suggestion to travel during shoulder seasons—when crowds were thinner and prices lower—fit her flexible schedule perfectly. She decided on a three-month road trip across the U.S., starting in the Northeast and working her way westward, with a focus on scenic routes and free or low-cost activities.

Cynthia's old hatchback, "Ruby," became her travel companion. The guidebook's advice on vehicle prep helped her get Ruby road-trip-ready: an oil change, new tires, and a roadside emergency kit. Feeling confident, Cynthia hit the road with a budget of $5,000, a cooler packed with snacks, and her United States Atlas Road Map Travel Guide riding shotgun.

Leg 1: The Northeast Charm

Cynthia's journey began in Maine, where the guidebook directed her to the Acadia National Park. She took the scenic Park Loop Road and marveled at the breathtaking coastline—all for the cost of a single park pass. The guide's local tips led her to a lobster shack on the outskirts of Bar Harbor, where she feasted on a fresh lobster roll without blowing her budget.

In Vermont, Cynthia followed the suggested route along the Kancamagus Highway, a winding road famous for its autumn foliage. She camped at a budget-friendly state park, using the guidebook's recommendation for campgrounds with showers and fire pits. Each evening, she planned the next day's adventures using the guide's detailed maps and tips.

Leg 2: The South's Warm Embrace

Heading south, Cynthia explored the historic streets of Charleston, South Carolina. The guidebook's walking tour map saved her from paying for pricey guided tours, and she discovered hidden gems like Rainbow Row and the Waterfront Park fountains. A local café, suggested in the dining section, offered her the best shrimp and grits she'd ever tasted.

In Florida, Cynthia followed the Overseas Highway to the Florida Keys, a drive the guidebook described as "a journey through turquoise waters and tropical breezes." To save money, she camped at a state park in Key Largo and spent her days snorkeling and exploring nature trails.

Leg 3: The Heart of the Midwest

In the Midwest, Cynthia embraced the simplicity of rural life. The guidebook's Hidden Gems section led her to the Great River Road, a route paralleling the Mississippi River. She stopped at small towns, sampled local pastries, and even joined a free town festival in Iowa, complete with live music and a pie-eating contest.

Chicago was her urban detour. The guidebook's advice on free attractions helped her explore Millennium Park, where she snapped a selfie in front of the famous Bean sculpture. Thanks to the guide's public transit tips, she navigated the city without the stress of parking fees.

Leg 4: The Majestic West

As Cynthia crossed into the West, her guidebook became indispensable. The National Parks Section detailed affordable ways to explore Yellowstone and Grand Teton National Park. She purchased an annual park pass, which paid for itself after visiting just a few parks.

On the Pacific Coast Highway, Cynthia drove with the windows down, the ocean breeze in her hair. The guidebook's suggested pull-off points led her to hidden beaches and scenic overlooks she might have missed otherwise.

In Utah, Cynthia explored the otherworldly landscapes of Arches National Park and Zion National Park. The guidebook's practical tips—like starting hikes early to avoid the midday heat—kept her safe and comfortable.

Staying on Budget

Cynthia credited her ability to stick to her budget to the guide's advice. She followed the section on budget-friendly dining by stopping at farmers' markets and cooking simple meals at campsites. The guidebook's list of free attractions, from public beaches to art installations, ensured her trip was rich in experiences without draining her wallet.

For accommodations, Cynthia alternated between budget motels, campsites, and the occasional stay with friends or family she met along the way. The guide's RV and Camping section helped her find well-maintained campgrounds with affordable rates.

A Life-Changing Journey

Three months later, Cynthia returned home with Ruby covered in road dust, her phone packed with photos, and her heart full of memories. She spent just under $4,800—proving that her dream road trip was not only possible but also well within her means.

Cynthia's journey inspired her friends, who eagerly borrowed her United States Atlas Road Map Travel Guide. The guide had not only made her trip seamless but had also shown her that adventure is accessible to anyone with the right tools and mindset.

Would you like to expand on any part of Cynthia's story or focus on a specific region or experience?

Embarking on a journey across the United States is an unparalleled adventure, one that invites travelers to immerse themselves in the vast diversity of landscapes, cultures, and experiences that define the nation. From the towering mountain ranges and sprawling plains to vibrant urban centers and quiet coastal towns, every corner of the country tells a story. For first-time visitors, navigating such an expansive destination can feel overwhelming, but with the right preparation, this epic road trip can transform into a series of unforgettable memories. Planning the trip is not just about marking destinations on a map; it's about understanding the spirit of each place and being ready to embrace what the journey unfolds.

The first step in preparing for such a journey involves equipping yourself with tools that simplify travel and enhance the experience. A reliable travel guide paired with a detailed road atlas is invaluable. It serves as a constant companion, providing step-by-step directions, highlighting noteworthy stops, and offering practical advice for traversing unfamiliar territories. The secret to a smooth road trip lies in blending structured plans with the flexibility to explore unplanned detours and hidden gems along the way.

Arriving in a new city can be both thrilling and daunting. For first-time travelers, it's essential to take a moment to familiarize yourself with the area. Start with a central point—a bustling downtown area, a well-known park, or a historic district—and use it as a base to explore further. Walking through the heart of a city offers an authentic glimpse into the local culture. It's here that you'll often find vibrant farmers' markets, cozy cafes filled with locals, and public spaces alive with the rhythm of daily life.

Driving into an unfamiliar city brings its own set of challenges. Traffic patterns, unfamiliar signs, and new road layouts can feel intimidating, but patience is your best ally. Take advantage of navigation tools while keeping an eye on landmarks to stay oriented. If you get the chance, stop at a visitor center or local tourism office; these spots are treasure troves of maps, brochures, and personalized recommendations.

Exploring the United States is not just about ticking off destinations on a list—it's about embracing the journey. The open road itself offers a canvas for reflection and discovery. Whether you're cruising along winding coastal highways, crossing vast stretches of desert, or weaving through forested mountain paths, the changing scenery creates an ever-evolving backdrop for your adventure. These quiet moments between destinations are often where the magic happens. A roadside diner with decades of history, a quaint general store, or a scenic overlook with no one else around can leave the most lasting impressions.

Accommodation options vary greatly depending on the region, and part of the adventure lies in discovering the perfect place to rest your head. While chain hotels offer consistency and convenience, local inns, family-owned motels, and charming bed-and-breakfasts provide a personal touch that larger establishments can't replicate. Campgrounds, whether in national parks or along quiet byways, allow travelers to connect with nature while keeping costs low. When selecting where to stay, seek out recommendations from locals or fellow travelers—they often lead to the most memorable spots.

Food is a journey in itself, revealing the unique heritage and traditions of each region. Whether it's fresh seafood along the New England coast, spicy Cajun dishes in Louisiana, or mouthwatering barbecue in Texas, every state boasts its own culinary treasures. Road trips offer the perfect opportunity to explore these flavors. Opt for locally owned restaurants, roadside diners, and food trucks to experience the best a region has to offer. Don't hesitate to ask locals about their favorite dishes or hidden dining spots—these conversations often lead to unexpected culinary delights.

Safety and preparedness are critical for a successful road trip. Weather conditions can vary dramatically from one state to another, so keeping an eye on forecasts and being ready for sudden changes is essential. Remote areas may have limited services, so it's wise to carry plenty of water, snacks, and a well-stocked first aid kit. Gas stations can be few and far between in certain parts of the country, especially in rural or desert regions, so refueling whenever you have the chance is a must. Ensuring your vehicle is in good condition before setting off—checking tire pressure, oil levels, and brakes—can save you from unexpected breakdowns.

One of the greatest joys of exploring the United States is meeting its people. Each town and city has its own personality, shaped by the locals who call it home. From friendly gas station attendants to enthusiastic tour guides, the individuals you meet along the way will enrich your experience with their stories and perspectives. Attend local festivals, markets, or community events to get a true sense of a place's character. Museums and galleries offer insight into its history and artistic expression, while parks and public spaces reveal the everyday life of its residents.

For travelers seeking budget-friendly options, the United States offers a wealth of affordable experiences. Many attractions, such as national parks, museums, and historic landmarks, are free or low-cost, especially if you plan ahead. Investing in an annual national park pass, for example, allows unlimited access to some of the most breathtaking natural wonders in the country. Exploring on foot or by bike not only saves money but also provides a closer connection to your surroundings. Additionally, traveling during off-peak seasons often means lower prices for accommodations and fewer crowds at popular destinations.

The diversity of the United States is reflected in its landscapes, cultures, and traditions, making every stop along your journey unique. Coastal areas invite you to dip your toes in the ocean or explore rugged cliffs. Mountain regions challenge you with winding trails and stunning vistas. Urban centers buzz with energy, offering an endless array of activities, while rural towns provide a peaceful escape. Each destination tells its own story, and by approaching your travels with curiosity and openness, you'll uncover layers of meaning and connection.

As your road trip unfolds, let the journey guide you. Be open to the unexpected, from a spontaneous detour to a conversation with a stranger. Take time to reflect on the landscapes you've crossed and the experiences you've gathered. Whether you're capturing these moments with a camera or simply holding them in your heart, they'll become the stories you tell long after the trip is over.

Traveling across the United States is more than a vacation—it's a transformative experience that leaves you with a deeper appreciation for the vastness and diversity of the world around you. With the right preparation, a spirit of adventure, and a reliable guide to lead the way, this journey becomes more than just a collection of destinations. It becomes a personal narrative, woven together by the people you meet, the roads you travel, and the places you discover. Every turn of the wheel, every step you take, adds to this incredible story, creating memories that last a lifetime.

CHAPTER 1
Welcome to the Ultimate Road Trip Guide

Embarking on a journey across the United States is an unparalleled adventure, one that invites travelers to immerse themselves in the vast diversity of landscapes, cultures, and experiences that define the nation. From the towering mountain ranges and sprawling plains to vibrant urban centers and quiet coastal towns, every corner of the country tells a story. For first-time visitors, navigating such an expansive destination can feel overwhelming, but with the right preparation, this epic road trip can transform into a series of unforgettable memories. Planning the trip is not just about marking destinations on a map; it's about understanding the spirit of each place and being ready to embrace what the journey unfolds.

The first step in preparing for such a journey involves equipping yourself with tools that simplify travel and enhance the experience. A reliable travel guide paired with a detailed road atlas is invaluable. It serves as a constant companion, providing step-by-step directions, highlighting noteworthy stops, and offering practical advice for traversing unfamiliar territories. The secret to a smooth road trip lies in blending structured plans with the flexibility to explore unplanned detours and hidden gems along the way.

Arriving in a new city can be both thrilling and daunting. For first-time travelers, it's essential to take a moment to familiarize yourself with the area. Start with a central point—a bustling downtown area, a well-known park, or a historic district—and use it as a base to explore further. Walking through the heart of a city offers an authentic glimpse into the local culture. It's here that you'll often find vibrant farmers' markets, cozy cafes filled with locals, and public spaces alive with the rhythm of daily life.

Driving into an unfamiliar city brings its own set of challenges. Traffic patterns, unfamiliar signs, and new road layouts can feel intimidating, but patience is your best ally. Take advantage of navigation tools while keeping an eye on landmarks to stay oriented. If you get the chance, stop at a visitor center or local tourism office; these spots are treasure troves of maps, brochures, and personalized recommendations.

Exploring the United States is not just about ticking off destinations on a list—it's about embracing the journey. The open road itself offers a canvas for reflection and discovery. Whether you're cruising along winding coastal highways, crossing vast stretches of desert, or weaving through forested mountain paths, the changing scenery creates an ever-evolving backdrop for your adventure. These quiet moments between destinations are often where the magic happens. A roadside diner with decades of history, a quaint general store, or a scenic overlook with no one else around can leave the most lasting impressions.

Accommodation options vary greatly depending on the region, and part of the adventure lies in discovering the perfect place to rest your head. While chain hotels offer consistency and convenience, local inns, family-owned motels, and charming bed-and-breakfasts provide a personal touch that larger establishments can't replicate. Campgrounds, whether in national parks or along quiet byways, allow travelers to connect with nature while keeping costs low. When selecting where to stay, seek out recommendations from locals or fellow travelers—they often lead to the most memorable spots.

Food is a journey in itself, revealing the unique heritage and traditions of each region. Whether it's fresh seafood along the New England coast, spicy Cajun dishes in Louisiana, or mouthwatering barbecue in Texas, every state boasts its own culinary treasures. Road trips offer the perfect opportunity to explore these flavors. Opt for locally owned restaurants, roadside diners, and food trucks to experience the best a region has to offer. Don't hesitate to ask locals about their favorite dishes or hidden dining spots—these conversations often lead to unexpected culinary delights.

Safety and preparedness are critical for a successful road trip. Weather conditions can vary dramatically from one state to another, so keeping an eye on forecasts and being ready for sudden changes is essential. Remote areas may have limited services, so it's wise to carry plenty of water, snacks, and a well-stocked first aid kit. Gas stations can be few and far between in certain parts of the country, especially in rural or desert regions, so refueling whenever you have the chance is a must. Ensuring your vehicle is in good condition before setting off—checking tire pressure, oil levels, and brakes—can save you from unexpected breakdowns.

One of the greatest joys of exploring the United States is meeting its people. Each town and city has its own personality, shaped by the locals who call it home. From friendly gas station attendants to enthusiastic tour guides, the individuals you meet along the way will enrich your experience with their stories and perspectives. Attend local festivals, markets, or community events to get a true sense of a place's character. Museums and galleries offer insight into its history and artistic expression, while parks and public spaces reveal the everyday life of its residents.

For travelers seeking budget-friendly options, the United States offers a wealth of affordable experiences. Many attractions, such as national parks, museums, and historic landmarks, are free or low-cost, especially if you plan ahead. Investing in an annual national park pass, for example, allows unlimited access to some of the most breathtaking natural wonders in the country. Exploring on foot or by bike not only saves money but also provides a closer connection to your surroundings. Additionally, traveling during off-peak seasons often means lower prices for accommodations and fewer crowds at popular destinations.

The diversity of the United States is reflected in its landscapes, cultures, and traditions, making every stop along your journey unique. Coastal areas invite you to dip your toes in the ocean or explore rugged cliffs. Mountain regions challenge you with winding trails and stunning vistas. Urban centers buzz with energy, offering an endless array of activities, while rural towns provide a peaceful escape. Each destination tells its own story, and by approaching your travels with curiosity and openness, you'll uncover layers of meaning and connection.

As your road trip unfolds, let the journey guide you. Be open to the unexpected, from a spontaneous detour to a conversation with a stranger. Take time to reflect on the landscapes you've crossed and the experiences you've gathered. Whether you're capturing these moments with a camera or simply holding them in your heart, they'll become the stories you tell long after the trip is over.

Traveling across the United States is more than a vacation—it's a transformative experience that leaves you with a deeper appreciation for the vastness and diversity of the world around you. With the right preparation, a spirit of adventure, and a reliable guide to lead the way, this journey becomes more than just a collection of destinations. It becomes a personal narrative, woven together by the people you meet, the roads you travel, and the places you discover. Every turn of the wheel, every step you take, adds to this incredible story, creating memories that last a lifetime.

Traveling through the United States on a road trip is a journey like no other, a chance to experience the sheer vastness and incredible diversity that defines the country. Each stretch of road unveils new landscapes, rich cultural traditions, and unexpected encounters. For first-time visitors, this grand adventure can seem overwhelming at first glance, but with careful preparation, an open mind, and the right tools, the journey can be not only manageable but immensely rewarding. Every mile you cover becomes a piece of a larger story, one that captures the unique essence of each destination along the way.

Planning is the backbone of any successful road trip. Start by familiarizing yourself with the routes you'll be taking, noting key landmarks, major highways, and scenic byways. A reliable road atlas paired with a comprehensive travel guide acts as your compass, ensuring you stay on track while allowing room for spontaneity. With these tools, even the most remote stretches of road can feel accessible. Preparation also includes making your vehicle road-ready. Checking tire pressure, oil levels, and brakes before hitting the road minimizes the risk of unexpected mechanical issues. Packing a roadside emergency kit, complete with jumper cables, a flashlight, and a spare tire, adds another layer of security.

Arriving in an unfamiliar city for the first time is an exhilarating experience. Each place has its own rhythm and personality, shaped by its geography, history, and the people who live there. The best way to begin exploring is by heading to a central location, such as a downtown district, a main plaza, or a local park. These areas often act as hubs of activity and provide a snapshot of the city's culture. Take a moment to observe your surroundings—the architecture, the sounds, the energy of the people—and let yourself be drawn into the flow of daily life.

Navigating new roads and cities can be intimidating, but it's a skill that becomes easier with practice. Digital navigation tools are invaluable for real-time updates and turn-by-turn directions, but a physical map provides a broader perspective, allowing you to see alternative routes and plan ahead. Combining these resources ensures that you're well-prepared, whether you're entering a bustling urban area or meandering through quiet country roads. Visitor centers and tourism offices are excellent places to stop for local advice, maps, and brochures that highlight nearby attractions.

The beauty of a road trip lies not just in the destinations but in the journey itself. Long stretches of highway become opportunities for reflection and discovery. Each region offers its own distinct character, from the rugged coastlines of the Pacific Northwest to the sunlit deserts of the Southwest. Along the way, roadside attractions, scenic overlooks, and quirky small towns add charm and variety to the experience. Don't rush through these moments—pause, take in the view, and allow the journey to unfold naturally.

Connecting with locals is one of the most enriching aspects of travel. Their insights often lead to discoveries you won't find in any guidebook—a hidden hiking trail, a hole-in-the-wall diner, or a little-known historical site. Engaging in conversations at coffee shops, farmers' markets, or gas stations opens the door to these unique experiences. People are often eager to share the best their community has to offer, especially with travelers who show genuine interest.

Accommodations during a road trip range from the familiar comfort of chain hotels to the rustic charm of campgrounds and family-owned inns. Each option brings its own set of advantages. While larger hotels offer predictable amenities, smaller establishments often provide a more personal touch, with hosts who are happy to share local tips and recommendations. Camping, particularly in national or state parks, offers a chance to wake up surrounded by natural beauty—a lake, a forest, or a mountain range just steps from your tent or RV.

Food is a gateway to understanding the culture of a place. The flavors of a region tell stories of its history, its people, and its traditions. Seek out locally owned restaurants, diners, and food trucks to experience authentic regional cuisine. From the lobster rolls of New England to the spicy Creole dishes of Louisiana, every stop offers a new culinary adventure. Farmers' markets and food festivals are also excellent places to sample fresh, local ingredients and meet the people who produce them.

Safety is a priority for any traveler, particularly when navigating unfamiliar territories. Weather can change rapidly, especially in mountainous or coastal areas, so keeping an eye on forecasts is crucial. Carrying extra water, snacks, and a well-stocked first aid kit ensures you're prepared for any situation. Gas stations can be sparse in rural regions, so filling up your tank regularly is a smart habit. Staying aware of local driving laws, speed limits, and road conditions helps avoid unnecessary complications.

The landscapes of the United States are as diverse as its people, offering a wide range of experiences that cater to every traveler's interests. Coastal regions invite you to explore beaches and cliffs, while mountainous areas challenge you with trails and breathtaking vistas. Urban centers buzz with activity, showcasing art, music, and innovation, while rural towns offer a slower pace and a chance to connect with nature. Each destination has its own story to tell, and the joy of a road trip lies in discovering those stories firsthand.

Budget-conscious travelers will find plenty of ways to save without sacrificing the quality of their experience. Many attractions, such as national parks, historic sites, and public festivals, are free or have minimal entrance fees. Purchasing an annual national park pass is a cost-effective way to access some of the country's most stunning natural wonders. Traveling during off-peak seasons not only lowers costs for accommodations and attractions but also provides a quieter, more relaxed experience.

As you travel, take time to appreciate the people and places that make each stop unique. Attend local events, visit museums and galleries, or simply spend time in public spaces observing the rhythms of everyday life. These experiences create a deeper connection to the places you visit, turning a simple trip into a meaningful journey. Every conversation, every meal, and every detour adds to the richness of your adventure.

A road trip across the United States is more than just a vacation—it's an exploration of the landscapes, cultures, and histories that make this country so extraordinary. With thoughtful preparation, a spirit of curiosity, and a willingness to embrace the unexpected, your journey becomes a story worth telling. Let the road guide you, let the people you meet inspire you, and let the destinations leave you with memories that will last a lifetime. Every stretch of highway, every turn of the wheel, and every stop along the way becomes a part of your narrative, a testament to the beauty of exploration and the joy of discovery.

CHAPTER 2
THE U.S

Traveling across the United States is an exhilarating experience, a journey through diverse terrains, unique cultural landscapes, and a rich tapestry of history. Every mile unfolds a new story, revealing hidden gems, iconic landmarks, and unexpected encounters that make the adventure unforgettable. For first-time visitors, the sheer size and variety of the country might seem overwhelming, but with proper planning and the right guide, this expansive road trip becomes a seamless and rewarding experience. Each destination, from bustling cities to serene natural retreats, offers its own unique charm, and every stretch of the journey is an opportunity to discover something new and enriching.

Preparation is the cornerstone of a successful road trip, and this guidebook is designed to be your ultimate companion on the road. Start by acquainting yourself with its layout and features, including detailed maps, insider tips, and practical advice tailored to every kind of traveler. Whether you're setting out for a cross-country adventure or exploring a single state, the structure of this book ensures you can easily find the information you need. Take a moment to familiarize yourself with the maps, which include key landmarks, scenic byways, and important services like rest stops and fuel stations. These maps, combined with step-by-step directions, make navigation simple and stress-free.

When beginning your journey, ensure your vehicle is ready for the road. A quick inspection of essential components like tire pressure, brakes, and oil levels can save you from unexpected delays. Packing a roadside emergency kit, complete with items like jumper cables, a flashlight, and a first-aid kit, adds an extra layer of security. For travelers using electric vehicles, planning charging stops along your route is equally important. These small steps ensure that your focus remains on the adventure ahead rather than on avoidable challenges.

As you set out, let the guidebook lead you to your first destination. Each section is thoughtfully designed to provide clear, layman-friendly directions, perfect for anyone navigating a new area for the first time. Whether you're driving through busy urban streets or winding rural roads, the detailed instructions keep you on track. For example, instead of vague landmarks, the guide emphasizes clear points of reference like specific exit numbers, notable buildings, or natural features that make navigation intuitive. It's like having a knowledgeable friend in the passenger seat, guiding you through every turn.

Arriving in a new town or city is a thrilling experience, especially for first-time visitors. Begin by heading to a central location like a historic district, a bustling plaza, or a popular park. These areas often act as the heart of the community, offering a glimpse into local life and culture. Step out of your vehicle, take a moment to absorb the atmosphere, and let the surroundings welcome you. Pay attention to the architecture, the rhythm of daily life, and the unique features that define the area. This initial exploration sets the tone for the rest of your visit.

Once you've oriented yourself, dive into the local attractions. The guidebook provides a curated list of must-visit spots, ranging from iconic landmarks to hidden gems known only to locals. For example, you might discover a scenic overlook tucked away from the main roads or a family-run restaurant serving recipes that have been passed down for generations. These recommendations are enriched with insights gathered from years of travel and conversations with residents, making each suggestion feel personal and authentic.

During your journey, embrace the moments between destinations. The roads themselves often hold surprises, from quirky roadside attractions to breathtaking natural vistas. Pull over at scenic rest stops to stretch your legs and take in the views. These pauses not only break up the drive but also give you a deeper appreciation for the landscapes you're traversing. Whether it's a colorful mural on the side of a building, a historic marker by the highway, or a charming small-town general store, these unplanned discoveries add richness to your experience.

Food is an integral part of any trip, and exploring regional cuisines is one of the joys of road travel. Use the guidebook to find local eateries, from cozy diners to food trucks and upscale restaurants. Each recommendation is selected to give you a taste of the area's culinary heritage, whether it's fresh seafood along the coast, hearty barbecue in the South, or handmade pasta in an Italian-American neighborhood. Don't hesitate to ask locals for their favorite spots—these conversations often lead to the most memorable meals.

Accommodations play a crucial role in shaping your journey. The guidebook offers a range of options to suit every budget and preference, from well-known hotel chains to unique stays like bed-and-breakfasts, historic inns, and campgrounds. Each suggestion includes practical details such as proximity to major attractions, available amenities, and tips for making the most of your stay. For those who enjoy the great outdoors, camping in national or state parks offers an immersive experience, with opportunities to wake up to stunning views and the sounds of nature.

Safety is a priority for any traveler, and the guidebook provides practical advice to keep your trip worry-free. Weather conditions can change rapidly, especially in mountainous or coastal areas, so staying informed and prepared is essential. Always carry extra water, snacks, and a charged phone with navigation apps downloaded for offline use. If your route takes you through remote regions, make sure to refuel frequently and keep an eye on your vehicle's condition. These simple precautions ensure peace of mind throughout your journey.

Connecting with locals is one of the most rewarding aspects of travel. Their stories and insights add depth to your experience, revealing aspects of a destination that you might otherwise miss. Strike up conversations at farmers' markets, coffee shops, or community events. You'll often learn about unique traditions, upcoming festivals, or little-known attractions that give the area its distinct character. These interactions create lasting memories and remind you of the shared humanity that connects us all.

The landscapes of the United States are as varied as they are beautiful, offering endless opportunities for exploration. Coastal areas invite you to stroll along sandy beaches or explore rocky cliffs, while mountainous regions challenge you with hiking trails and panoramic views. Urban centers pulse with energy, showcasing art, music, and innovation, while rural towns offer a quieter pace and a chance to connect with nature. Each destination tells its own story, and this guidebook helps you uncover those narratives, turning a simple trip into an unforgettable adventure.

Budget-conscious travelers will appreciate the guidebook's emphasis on affordable experiences. Many attractions, such as national parks, historic sites, and public festivals, offer free or low-cost entry. Traveling during off-peak seasons not only saves money but also provides a more relaxed experience, free from large crowds. Simple tips like packing your own snacks, cooking meals at campsites, and taking advantage of free attractions help stretch your budget without compromising the quality of your trip.

As you journey through the pages of this guidebook and the roads of the United States, let curiosity lead the way. Each chapter, map, and recommendation is designed to inspire and empower you, making every step of your adventure seamless and enriching. The road ahead is full of possibilities, and this guide is here to ensure you make the most of every mile. Let the journey begin, and let it transform the way you see the world and yourself.

CHAPTER 3
Why Explore the U.S. by Road

Exploring the United States during 2025-2026 is an opportunity to experience the full breadth of a country that has something to offer for every kind of traveler. From its iconic landmarks to its hidden treasures, every journey across its vast landscapes reveals a patchwork of cultures, histories, and natural wonders. Whether you're planning to drive along the scenic Pacific Coast Highway, immerse yourself in the vibrant rhythms of a bustling city, or lose yourself in the tranquility of remote national parks, this guidebook is your key to unlocking the adventure of a lifetime. Traveling here isn't just about seeing new places—it's about connecting with the people, traditions, and stories that make each destination unique.

Before setting out, the first step is to determine the kind of journey you want to embark on. Are you drawn to the energy of cities, where every corner bursts with culture, art, and food? Or perhaps you prefer the stillness of nature, where you can hike through untouched wilderness or sit by a serene lake? By defining your priorities, you can create a flexible itinerary that ensures you make the most of your time on the road. This guide will help you plan those details, offering suggestions for routes, stops, and activities that align with your interests.

Imagine the thrill of beginning your journey in the Northeast, where centuries-old cities like Boston and Philadelphia whisper stories of the nation's founding. Walking through cobblestone streets and alongside towering colonial-era buildings, you'll feel as though you've stepped back in time. The changing seasons bring an added layer of beauty, with autumn transforming the region into a canvas of red, orange, and gold. Beyond the cities, smaller towns offer quieter charms. Stroll through covered bridges, enjoy a steaming bowl of clam chowder at a family-owned diner, or visit historical landmarks that transport you to pivotal moments in American history.

As you move south, you'll feel the warmth of Southern hospitality enveloping you. From the laid-back coastal vibes of Charleston to the electric nightlife of Nashville, the South offers an array of experiences that appeal to every traveler. Follow the smell of barbecue through the streets of Memphis, or enjoy the rolling hills of Virginia's wine country. The region's rich history is evident in its grand plantations, Civil Rights landmarks, and well-preserved Civil War battlefields. Take the time to talk with locals—they're often eager to share personal stories and recommend their favorite hidden spots.

In the Midwest, the vast openness of the landscape offers a calming change of pace. Known as the heartland of America, this region is filled with endless possibilities for adventure. Picture yourself driving past golden fields of wheat that sway in the breeze, stopping at quirky roadside attractions like the World's Largest Ball of Twine, or sampling world-class Chicago-style pizza in the Windy City. The Great Lakes are a treasure trove of natural beauty, where you can explore sandy beaches, kayak along crystal-clear waters, or hike trails surrounded by lush greenery. Small-town festivals and farmers' markets bring communities together, offering travelers a taste of the local way of life.

Heading westward, the dramatic scenery of the Rockies and the expansive deserts of the Southwest greet you with open arms. Whether it's gazing at the grandeur of the Grand Canyon, walking among the red rock formations of Arches National Park, or enjoying the crisp mountain air in Colorado, the western United States showcases some of the most breathtaking landscapes in the world. The region also offers a vibrant cultural experience, with its blend of Native American heritage, cowboy traditions, and modern art scenes. Explore historic mining towns, dine at roadside diners where time seems to stand still, or stargaze in some of the darkest skies you'll ever encounter.

Finally, the Pacific Coast provides a dazzling contrast to the interior of the country. Drive along the edge of the continent, where rugged cliffs meet the crashing waves of the Pacific Ocean. Stop in

San Francisco for a stroll across the Golden Gate Bridge, visit wine country in California's Napa Valley, or relax on the beaches of Santa Monica. Further north, the forests of Oregon and Washington offer an entirely different kind of beauty, with towering trees, cascading waterfalls, and cozy small towns that feel like home. The seafood here is a highlight, with fresh-caught salmon, Dungeness crab, and oysters waiting to be savored.

Throughout your journey, use this guidebook to enhance your experience. Each section is carefully designed to help you navigate new places with ease. From maps that highlight the best routes to insider tips on avoiding crowds at popular attractions, this book is your trusted travel companion. For instance, if you're visiting Yellowstone National Park, the guide might suggest arriving early in the morning to see the geysers without the midday rush. If you're in New Orleans, it might point you toward a lesser-known jazz club where the music is just as magical as the famous spots.

One of the most rewarding aspects of travel is the opportunity to immerse yourself in local life. Stop at roadside diners where waitresses call you "hun," explore neighborhood markets filled with handmade crafts, or attend a local event like a town parade or a seasonal festival. These moments give you a glimpse into the everyday lives of the people who call these places home. They also create lasting memories—ones that can't be found on the pages of a guidebook but are born from genuine human connection.

Practicality is a core element of this guide, ensuring that first-time visitors feel confident and prepared at every step. Before hitting the road, review the checklist of essentials to pack, including a fully stocked first-aid kit, a reusable water bottle, and snacks to keep you fueled between stops. Familiarize yourself with basic road safety tips, such as how to handle sudden weather changes or what to do if your car breaks down in a remote area. Knowing these small but important details allows you to focus on the joy of exploration.

The diversity of the United States means that every day on the road brings something new. Perhaps you'll wake up to the sound of waves crashing against the shore, spend the afternoon exploring a bustling city, and end the day watching a fiery sunset over a desert landscape. These contrasts are what make traveling here so captivating. Each region tells its own story, shaped by its geography, culture, and history. By the time your journey comes to an end, you'll have collected not just souvenirs but also a wealth of experiences that remind you of the beauty and complexity of the world.

Traveling the United States in 2025-2026 is not just about visiting places—it's about creating connections, learning from the past, and embracing the present. The roads you take, the people you meet, and the moments you share become part of a larger narrative, one that reflects the spirit of adventure and the joy of discovery. Let this guide be your roadmap, your inspiration, and your companion as you explore the highways and byways of this extraordinary country. The journey is yours to shape, and the memories you create will last a lifetime.

CHAPTER 4
Essential Packing Tips for Road Travelers

When preparing for a road trip across the United States, packing becomes more than just a chore; it's an essential part of ensuring your journey is both enjoyable and stress-free. The success of any road adventure often hinges on the items you bring along, and having the right essentials within reach can make a huge difference when exploring new destinations. Whether you're heading out for a weekend getaway or a months-long cross-country expedition, every item in your bag serves a purpose, helping you navigate unexpected challenges, stay comfortable, and fully embrace the adventure ahead.

To start, think of the foundation of your trip: the documents and tools that make everything run smoothly. Always ensure you have your driver's license, vehicle registration, and proof of insurance stored safely but readily accessible, such as in the glove compartment. Having these documents at hand can save valuable time during routine checks or unexpected situations. A hard copy of a comprehensive road atlas is a smart addition—while GPS apps are convenient, they rely on cell service, which might be limited in remote areas. A printed map not only acts as a reliable backup but also provides a broader perspective of the areas you're traveling through, allowing you to spot alternative routes or hidden scenic roads.

When it comes to personal items, consider the practicalities of what you'll need for both comfort and function. Pack a variety of clothing that's suited to the climates you'll be passing through. Layering is a traveler's best friend, as it allows you to adjust easily to changing weather. Lightweight, moisture-wicking fabrics work well for warm weather, while a cozy fleece or insulated jacket is essential for colder regions or nighttime temperatures. Footwear should be versatile and comfortable—bring a sturdy pair for outdoor adventures, casual shoes for city strolls, and perhaps flip-flops for quick stops or beach days. Organizing your clothing with packing cubes helps keep everything tidy and accessible, especially when living out of a suitcase or backpack for days at a time.

Staying nourished and hydrated on the road is crucial, particularly when driving through long stretches without easy access to food or water. Pack a sturdy cooler stocked with snacks that travel well, such as nuts, dried fruits, granola bars, and pre-cut vegetables. These can keep hunger at bay during extended drives and help you avoid relying on fast food or convenience store options. A reusable water bottle is an absolute must, not just for hydration but also to minimize plastic waste. Many rest stops and public spaces now offer refill stations, making it easy to keep your bottle topped up throughout the day.

Safety should always remain at the forefront of your planning. Assemble a roadside emergency kit tailored to the specifics of your trip. For instance, if you're heading into snowy regions, include items like a snow scraper and tire chains. Basic essentials such as jumper cables, a flashlight with spare batteries, and a tire repair kit are indispensable no matter where you're traveling. A first-aid kit should include adhesive bandages, antiseptic wipes, over-the-counter pain relievers, and any prescription medications you require. On one particularly memorable trip through the Arizona desert, having a fully stocked kit came in handy when we faced unexpected challenges due to the rugged terrain.

Entertainment is another key factor in making the journey enjoyable, especially on long drives or during downtime. Audiobooks, podcasts, and curated playlists can make the miles fly by, while travel games or puzzles keep passengers entertained. For those who enjoy photography, a good camera or even a smartphone with ample storage allows you to capture the landscapes, landmarks, and candid moments you'll encounter along the way. Portable power banks ensure your devices stay charged, while a Bluetooth speaker adds a fun touch for outdoor picnics or campsites.

The unpredictability of weather across the United States means you'll need to be prepared for anything. A compact rain jacket or umbrella is essential for sudden showers, while sunscreen and a hat protect you during sunny outdoor activities. If you're heading into colder climates, gloves and a warm hat are necessary to stay comfortable. During one of my winter trips to the Rockies, a thermal blanket and hand warmers were invaluable, providing warmth during a chilly evening when the temperatures dropped more than expected.

Packing versatile items that serve multiple purposes can also save space and add convenience. Reusable Ziploc bags are handy for storing snacks, keeping electronics dry, or even holding laundry. Duct tape is a surprisingly useful addition, capable of quick fixes from sealing a torn bag to making temporary repairs on your gear. A microfiber towel is lightweight, compact, and dries quickly, making it ideal for anything from impromptu swims to wiping down surfaces.

Think about the experiences you want to have during your trip and pack accordingly. If you plan to hike, bring a pair of binoculars for wildlife spotting and a lightweight daypack for carrying water, snacks, and sunscreen. For those heading to the beach, pack a foldable chair, a waterproof phone pouch, and a quick-drying towel. On a recent trip to the Florida Keys, having a small portable fan and a cooling towel made the hot, humid afternoons much more comfortable.

Staying organized is the key to reducing stress on the road. Keep frequently used items like snacks, maps, and chargers within easy reach, ideally in a bag or organizer near the driver's seat. Store less urgent supplies, such as extra clothing or backup gear, in the trunk or a roof-mounted cargo carrier. Labeling or color-coding your bags can help you find what you need quickly, especially when traveling with others.

Finally, pack with an eye toward sustainability. Use reusable containers for snacks, avoid single-use plastic bags, and opt for eco-friendly toiletries. Many national parks and public spaces have strict guidelines about minimizing waste, so being prepared with the right gear not only helps the environment but also keeps you in compliance with local rules.

Thoughtful packing transforms a road trip into a smoother, more enjoyable experience, allowing you to focus on the adventure rather than worrying about what you might have forgotten. With each carefully chosen item, you're not just preparing for the road ahead—you're setting yourself up to fully immerse in the journey, ready to embrace every twist, turn, and unexpected moment along the way.

CHAPTER 5
Staying Safe and Healthy on the Road

Staying safe and maintaining good health while traveling across the United States is a cornerstone of an enjoyable and memorable journey. The first step to achieving this is understanding the unique conditions of the destinations you plan to visit. From local climates to cultural norms, knowing what to expect can significantly minimize challenges. Pack versatile clothing suitable for changing weather conditions and ensure you have a travel-friendly first aid kit. Include essentials such as adhesive bandages, antiseptic wipes, over-the-counter painkillers, and any prescription medications. If you have dietary restrictions or allergies, prepare by researching restaurants, grocery stores, or local food options in advance to avoid unexpected issues.

Safe transportation is essential during any journey. For those renting a vehicle, conduct a detailed inspection to confirm the car is in proper working condition, with all safety features like seat belts and brakes functioning well. Take regular breaks to prevent fatigue during long drives, and try to avoid traveling late at night, especially in areas you are unfamiliar with. If public transport is your choice, remain vigilant about your belongings, particularly in crowded spaces such as bus terminals or subway stations. Always keep copies of your essential travel documents, such as passports or identification cards, in a secure but accessible location.

Food safety is another critical factor. To avoid gastrointestinal issues, stick to reputable dining establishments and exercise caution when consuming street food, particularly in areas where food handling may be questionable. Drinking enough water is equally important. Carry a refillable water bottle to stay hydrated, especially in hotter climates or during physically demanding activities like hiking. When exploring remote regions, always ensure you have adequate food and water supplies and be equipped with a reliable navigation tool, whether it's a GPS device or an old-fashioned map.

Choosing accommodations wisely can make or break your trip. Before booking a hotel or rental property, read reviews to assess the safety of the neighborhood and the quality of the property's amenities. Upon arrival, familiarize yourself with emergency exits and verify room safety features like locks and smoke detectors. Solo travelers may want to prioritize accommodations in busier areas where there is more foot traffic, as this often indicates a higher level of security. Families and groups should look for lodging options in well-lit areas with easy access to local attractions or transportation.

While out and about, staying vigilant is key. Avoid isolated areas, particularly after sunset, and stick to well-populated paths. Engaging with locals can provide valuable insights into staying safe. For instance, they can highlight neighborhoods to avoid or offer tips on navigating public spaces. In regions near water, local advice on tides and currents can be lifesaving. Similarly, in mountain areas, locals may warn you about trail conditions or wildlife hazards that are not immediately apparent.

Maintaining your health during a trip is equally important. Before traveling, ensure you have any necessary vaccinations for the region you plan to visit. Seasonal vaccines, such as flu shots, might also be a good idea, depending on the time of year. If you are prone to motion sickness or other travel-related discomforts, pack remedies such as ginger chews or anti-nausea medications. Regular handwashing and the use of hand sanitizers can help prevent common illnesses. Balanced meals, adequate sleep, and staying active will keep your energy levels up, ensuring you can fully enjoy your adventures.

Respecting local customs and traditions enriches your travel experience while fostering positive interactions with residents. Be mindful of dress codes, social norms, and behaviors that may differ from your own. If you're unsure, asking locals or conducting light research beforehand can prevent misunderstandings. Small gestures, such as using local greetings or observing customary practices, can open doors to deeper cultural connections.

Technology can be a traveler's best friend, but it's wise to prepare for scenarios where you might lose connectivity. Download maps or guides for offline use and keep a physical copy of key information, such as hotel addresses and emergency contacts. If you're traveling abroad, familiarize yourself with the contact details for your country's embassy or consulate and save local emergency numbers. For those embarking on road trips, keep a paper map handy and learn basic navigation skills in case GPS systems fail.

Being prepared for unforeseen circumstances can transform potential setbacks into manageable inconveniences. Whether it's an unexpected weather event, a canceled flight, or minor illnesses, having a flexible mindset and a backup plan can make all the difference. Comprehensive travel insurance covering medical emergencies and trip disruptions is a smart investment. If traveling with companions, establish a meeting point in case you get separated. Solo travelers should frequently check in with someone back home, sharing updates and plans for added peace of mind.

Building rapport with locals is one of the most rewarding aspects of travel. Their recommendations often lead to hidden gems, from hole-in-the-wall restaurants to less-traveled scenic spots. Engaging respectfully and showing genuine interest in their way of life often results in warm and enriching exchanges. Even a simple smile or friendly greeting can foster goodwill and create opportunities to learn more about the community.

For destinations where the language barrier is significant, a little preparation goes a long way. Learning a handful of useful phrases, such as greetings, directions, or questions about food and transport, can help immensely. Using translation apps or carrying a small phrasebook can bridge communication gaps in more complex situations. Remember, patience and open body language are universally understood.

Outdoor enthusiasts should approach their adventures with care and preparation. Appropriate gear, such as sturdy footwear and layered clothing, ensures you're ready for changing weather or terrain. Always inform someone of your plans before setting off on a hike or nature exploration and stick to designated trails to reduce risks. If wildlife is a concern, research how to handle potential encounters responsibly. For instance, understanding whether to stay quiet or make noise in the presence of certain animals can be vital.

Traveling across the diverse landscapes of the United States offers unparalleled opportunities to experience a variety of cultures, histories, and natural wonders. From the bustling streets of metropolitan areas to the serene beauty of national parks, every corner has its own unique charm. By staying mindful of safety and health, you'll not only protect yourself but also enhance your ability to fully immerse in the journey. Keeping a flexible attitude and being well-prepared ensures that even the unexpected becomes a cherished part of your adventure. Stay open to the spontaneity of travel, as those unplanned moments often leave the most lasting impressions.

CHAPTER 6
Planning Your Journey

Planning a road trip across the United States is an exhilarating way to experience the country's varied landscapes, vibrant cultures, and unique attractions. To make the most of this adventure, thorough preparation is essential. Begin by deciding the main purpose of your journey. Are you chasing coastal breezes, mountain air, bustling cities, or quiet rural retreats? Identifying your priorities will help shape your itinerary. Once you have a vision, explore maps and online resources to draft a potential route. Keep flexibility in mind—sometimes the most memorable experiences come from unplanned detours.

Selecting your route is where the excitement begins. For efficiency, major highways and interstates are convenient, but to truly soak in the beauty of the journey, consider weaving in scenic routes. For instance, cruising along California's Pacific Coast Highway offers jaw-dropping ocean views, while the Great River Road along the Mississippi introduces you to charming river towns. Balancing practicality with discovery allows you to enjoy the convenience of main roads while embracing the charm of less-traveled paths.

Budgeting is one of the most important steps in planning any trip. Begin by calculating fuel expenses, taking into account your vehicle's mileage and the current gas prices in the states you'll be visiting. Accommodation costs can vary widely based on your preferences. Camping is often budget-friendly and connects you with nature, while mid-range motels or boutique inns provide comfort without breaking the bank. Set aside funds for meals and snacks, and don't forget to include a little extra for unexpected expenses, such as entry fees to attractions or roadside assistance, if needed.

Weather plays a significant role in shaping your journey. The vast geography of the United States means that weather conditions can vary dramatically depending on the time of year and the region you're exploring. For example, spring in the Southwest offers mild days perfect for hiking, while autumn in New England showcases breathtaking foliage. On the other hand, winter in the northern states may bring snowstorms, requiring special preparations like snow chains or all-weather tires. Checking weather updates regularly and planning accordingly ensures a smoother trip.

Preparation for emergencies is equally crucial. Equip your vehicle with an emergency kit containing items like jumper cables, a flashlight, a first-aid kit, and basic tools. A spare tire and a portable air compressor can be lifesavers if you encounter a flat tire far from the nearest service station. Make sure your vehicle undergoes a thorough inspection before you hit the road. Regular maintenance of brakes, tires, and fluids minimizes the likelihood of breakdowns. Additionally, keeping a roadside assistance plan provides peace of mind in case of unexpected situations.

To enhance your travel experience, immerse yourself in the local culture of the regions you pass through. Each state and city has its own flavor, from the barbecue traditions of Texas to the jazz scene of New Orleans. Ask locals for recommendations—they often know the best places to eat, scenic viewpoints, and attractions that are off the beaten path. These interactions can lead to unforgettable experiences, such as discovering a hidden diner with exceptional food or attending a community event that's not listed in any guidebook.

Accommodation options add a layer of adventure to your road trip. While hotels and motels are reliable, consider mixing in more unique stays like vacation rentals, cabins, or even overnight camping in national parks.

Waking up to the sunrise over a canyon or falling asleep under a sky full of stars creates moments that are hard to replicate in urban settings. Always book in advance when traveling during peak seasons to secure your preferred options.

Food is a cornerstone of any great journey. From grabbing a quick snack at a roadside diner to indulging in a gourmet meal at a local restaurant, your choices tell a story about the places you visit. Stocking a cooler with fruits, sandwiches, and drinks is a practical way to keep costs down and avoid hunger during long stretches between towns. When you arrive at your destination, don't shy away from trying regional specialties—these culinary delights are often a highlight of the trip.

Staying active and healthy on the road is vital to keeping spirits high. Plan regular stops to stretch your legs and recharge, particularly during long drives. Rest areas and parks are great for this purpose and often have picnic tables where you can relax and enjoy a meal. Staying hydrated is equally important, so carry a refillable water bottle and keep it handy. If you or your travel companions have medical conditions, pack sufficient medication and a list of nearby pharmacies along your route.

Interacting with locals often leads to the most enriching travel experiences. Whether it's chatting with a shop owner or attending a local farmers' market, these encounters add depth to your journey. You might learn about a little-known hiking trail or a cultural festival happening nearby. Showing genuine interest and respect goes a long way in creating meaningful connections.

For families and pet owners, special considerations can make the trip smoother. Keeping children entertained with games, books, or tablets prevents boredom during long stretches. Pets, on the other hand, require their own set of essentials, including food, water, and toys. Planning your stops at pet-friendly parks or accommodations ensures everyone in the family enjoys the trip.

Technology is an invaluable tool for modern travelers, but it's wise to have backup plans. Download offline maps, as GPS signals can be unreliable in remote areas. Keep a physical list of important addresses and phone numbers, and learn how to read a paper map in case of emergencies. If you're venturing into rural or wilderness areas, a satellite phone or two-way radio can be a lifesaver when cell service is unavailable.

As you navigate the vast landscapes of the United States, take time to appreciate the diversity around you. The towering peaks of the Rockies, the rolling fields of the Midwest, the sun-soaked beaches of Florida—all offer their own unique allure. Capture these moments through photos or journaling to preserve memories. Sharing your experiences with friends and family might inspire them to embark on their own adventures.

Flexibility is one of the greatest assets a traveler can have. While planning is essential, leaving room for spontaneity often leads to the most rewarding experiences. Whether it's taking an unexpected detour to explore a charming small town or stopping to watch the sunset over a quiet lake, these moments are often the ones you'll treasure most. A road trip isn't just about reaching a destination—it's about embracing the journey and everything it has to offer.

CHAPTER 7
Navigating the United States

Embarking on a journey across the United States offers an unparalleled opportunity to experience the nation's diverse regions and cultures. Proper preparation is key to navigating successfully, especially when using an atlas as your primary guide. An atlas provides a reliable backup to digital tools and a tactile way to explore, but understanding its layout and functionality is crucial for first-time travelers. Begin by familiarizing yourself with the symbols and features used in the maps, as these details will help you efficiently plan and execute your trip.

Maps are often divided by state or region, with detailed grids to pinpoint cities, highways, and landmarks. Learning to interpret these grids is essential for efficient navigation. Symbols often represent rest stops, fuel stations, scenic routes, and tourist attractions. Understanding the meaning of these icons allows you to anticipate your journey's needs, from locating gas stations in remote areas to finding a perfect picnic spot on a scenic byway. Elevation lines, another common feature, help identify challenging routes, such as steep mountain roads that may require extra caution.

Before hitting the road, it's essential to understand the driving laws and traffic rules specific to each state. While some regulations are consistent nationwide, others differ significantly and could impact your travel plans. For instance, speed limits can vary widely depending on the type of road and its location. Rural highways might allow higher speeds than urban areas, but sharp reductions near small towns are common. Cellphone use while driving is another area of variance, with many states enforcing strict hands-free laws. Familiarizing yourself with these details before you travel helps avoid penalties and ensures a safer journey.

One of the most beneficial aspects of using an atlas is its reliability in areas where digital navigation tools may fail. Remote regions often lack stable internet or cellular connections, and relying on GPS alone can be risky. Carrying a well-organized atlas provides peace of mind, allowing you to navigate confidently even in the most isolated parts of the country. Pairing the atlas with a basic compass ensures you stay oriented, particularly in wilderness areas or along unfamiliar rural routes.

Exploring scenic routes adds a layer of magic to any road trip. Unlike major highways designed for speed, these roads wind through picturesque landscapes and offer unique experiences that can't be found elsewhere. For instance, the Natchez Trace Parkway takes you through historic sites and lush forests in the Deep South, while the

Going-to-the-Sun Road in Montana reveals breathtaking vistas of Glacier National Park. These routes often have slower speed limits, so plan extra time to savor the journey and explore local attractions along the way.

Urban exploration can be daunting for first-time visitors, especially in major cities where traffic and parking present challenges. City maps in an atlas are invaluable, highlighting key streets, parking facilities, and public transit options. Reviewing these maps in advance allows you to identify safe and convenient places to park your car before navigating the city on foot or via transit. Many city maps also include areas of cultural or historical significance, helping you plan your sightseeing efficiently.

Local insights are invaluable for enhancing your road trip experience. Engaging with residents often uncovers hidden gems that aren't marked on any map. A casual chat at a roadside diner might lead to recommendations for the best local hiking trails or a charming farmers' market. These interactions enrich your journey, providing a deeper connection to the places you visit and a better understanding of their unique character.

Preparation for emergencies is a vital component of any travel plan. Equip your vehicle with a comprehensive emergency kit that includes jumper cables, a flashlight, basic tools, and a first-aid kit. A spare tire, tire iron, and portable air pump are also essential, especially when traveling long distances through rural or isolated areas. Before setting out, have a mechanic inspect your vehicle to ensure it's roadworthy. Regular maintenance checks on brakes, fluids, and tires minimize the risk of breakdowns and contribute to a stress-free journey.

Weather considerations can significantly influence your route and schedule. The United States spans several climate zones, meaning conditions can vary drastically within a single trip. For example, summer heatwaves in the Southwest may require extra hydration and vehicle cooling precautions, while winter travel in northern states demands preparedness for snow and ice. Keep an eye on local weather forecasts and have alternate routes in mind should road closures or severe weather disrupt your plans.

Finding accommodations that suit your preferences and budget is another important aspect of trip planning. From luxury hotels to rustic campgrounds, the United States offers a wide range of options. Researching in advance allows you to secure reservations in popular areas, especially during peak travel seasons. National and state parks often provide unique lodging opportunities, such as cabins or campgrounds with stunning views. Staying in these locations not only connects you with nature but also supports local conservation efforts.

Food is a cornerstone of any road trip experience. Sampling regional cuisine offers a window into the local culture and traditions of the places you visit. From fresh lobster rolls in New England to barbecue in Texas, each region has its own culinary highlights. While dining out is part of the adventure, stocking a cooler with snacks and beverages ensures you're prepared for long stretches between restaurants or grocery stores. Farmers' markets and roadside stands are excellent places to discover fresh, local produce and unique treats.

For families and pet owners, additional planning ensures everyone enjoys the trip. Keep children entertained with games, music, or educational activities that relate to the areas you're visiting. For pets, plan regular stops at parks or pet-friendly attractions to let them stretch and play. Always carry essentials like food, water, and any required medications for both children and pets.

Rest stops play an important role in long-distance travel. These facilities provide much-needed breaks to stretch your legs, use the restroom, and refuel. Some states offer rest areas equipped with picnic tables, vending machines, and pet areas, while others might have more basic amenities. Knowing where these stops are located along your route helps you plan your travel days more effectively.

Flexibility is key to a successful road trip. While it's important to have a general itinerary, leaving room for spontaneous detours often leads to the most memorable experiences. Whether it's a roadside attraction, a scenic overlook, or a small-town festival, these unplanned moments add richness to your journey. Embracing the unexpected fosters a sense of adventure and creates stories you'll cherish long after the trip is over.

Navigating the vast and varied landscapes of the United States requires preparation, curiosity, and a willingness to adapt. By combining the reliability of an atlas with thoughtful planning and local insights, you can create a travel experience that's both seamless and unforgettable. Each mile offers something new to discover, from awe-inspiring natural wonders to the vibrant cultures that make every region unique. With the right mindset and tools, your road trip will become a journey of discovery, connection, and lasting memories.

CHAPTER 8

Staying safe and maintaining good health while traveling across the United States is a cornerstone of an enjoyable and memorable journey. The first step to achieving this is understanding the unique conditions of the destinations you plan to visit. From local climates to cultural norms, knowing what to expect can significantly minimize challenges. Pack versatile clothing suitable for changing weather conditions and ensure you have a travel-friendly first aid kit. Include essentials such as adhesive bandages, antiseptic wipes, over-the-counter painkillers, and any prescription medications. If you have dietary restrictions or allergies, prepare by researching restaurants, grocery stores, or local food options in advance to avoid unexpected issues.

Safe transportation is essential during any journey. For those renting a vehicle, conduct a detailed inspection to confirm the car is in proper working condition, with all safety features like seat belts and brakes functioning well. Take regular breaks to prevent fatigue during long drives, and try to avoid traveling late at night, especially in areas you are unfamiliar with. If public transport is your choice, remain vigilant about your belongings, particularly in crowded spaces such as bus terminals or subway stations. Always keep copies of your essential travel documents, such as passports or identification cards, in a secure but accessible location.

Food safety is another critical factor. To avoid gastrointestinal issues, stick to reputable dining establishments and exercise caution when consuming street food, particularly in areas where food handling may be questionable. Drinking enough water is equally important. Carry a refillable water bottle to stay hydrated, especially in hotter climates or during physically demanding activities like hiking. When exploring remote regions, always ensure you have adequate food and water supplies and be equipped with a reliable navigation tool, whether it's a GPS device or an old-fashioned map.

Choosing accommodations wisely can make or break your trip. Before booking a hotel or rental property, read reviews to assess the safety of the neighborhood and the quality of the property's amenities. Upon arrival, familiarize yourself with emergency exits and verify room safety features like locks and smoke detectors. Solo travelers may want to prioritize accommodations in busier areas where there is more foot traffic, as this often indicates a higher level of security. Families and groups should look for lodging options in well-lit areas with easy access to local attractions or transportation.

While out and about, staying vigilant is key. Avoid isolated areas, particularly after sunset, and stick to well-populated paths. Engaging with locals can provide valuable insights into staying safe. For instance, they can highlight neighborhoods to avoid or offer tips on navigating public spaces. In regions near water, local advice on tides and currents can be lifesaving. Similarly, in mountain areas, locals may warn you about trail conditions or wildlife hazards that are not immediately apparent.

Maintaining your health during a trip is equally important. Before traveling, ensure you have any necessary vaccinations for the region you plan to visit. Seasonal vaccines, such as flu shots, might also be a good idea, depending on the time of year. If you are prone to motion sickness or other travel-related discomforts, pack remedies such as ginger chews or anti-nausea medications. Regular handwashing and the use of hand sanitizers can help prevent common illnesses. Balanced meals, adequate sleep, and staying active will keep your energy levels up, ensuring you can fully enjoy your adventures.

Respecting local customs and traditions enriches your travel experience while fostering positive interactions with residents. Be mindful of dress codes, social norms, and behaviors that may differ from your own. If you're unsure, asking locals or conducting light research beforehand can prevent misunderstandings. Small gestures, such as using local greetings or observing customary practices, can open doors to deeper cultural connections.

Technology can be a traveler's best friend, but it's wise to prepare for scenarios where you might lose connectivity. Download maps or guides for offline use and keep a physical copy of key information, such as hotel addresses and emergency contacts. If you're traveling abroad, familiarize yourself with the contact details for your country's embassy or consulate and save local emergency numbers. For those embarking on road trips, keep a paper map handy and learn basic navigation skills in case GPS systems fail.

Being prepared for unforeseen circumstances can transform potential setbacks into manageable inconveniences. Whether it's an unexpected weather event, a canceled flight, or minor illnesses, having a flexible mindset and a backup plan can make all the difference. Comprehensive travel insurance covering medical emergencies and trip disruptions is a smart investment. If traveling with companions, establish a meeting point in case you get separated. Solo travelers should frequently check in with someone back home, sharing updates and plans for added peace of mind.

Building rapport with locals is one of the most rewarding aspects of travel. Their recommendations often lead to hidden gems, from hole-in-the-wall restaurants to less-traveled scenic spots. Engaging respectfully and showing genuine interest in their way of life often results in warm and enriching exchanges. Even a simple smile or friendly greeting can foster goodwill and create opportunities to learn more about the community.

For destinations where the language barrier is significant, a little preparation goes a long way. Learning a handful of useful phrases, such as greetings, directions, or questions about food and transport, can help immensely. Using translation apps or carrying a small phrasebook can bridge communication gaps in more complex situations. Remember, patience and open body language are universally understood.

Outdoor enthusiasts should approach their adventures with care and preparation. Appropriate gear, such as sturdy footwear and layered clothing, ensures you're ready for changing weather or terrain. Always inform someone of your plans before setting off on a hike or nature exploration and stick to designated trails to reduce risks. If wildlife is a concern, research how to handle potential encounters responsibly. For instance, understanding whether to stay quiet or make noise in the presence of certain animals can be vital.

Traveling across the diverse landscapes of the United States offers unparalleled opportunities to experience a variety of cultures, histories, and natural wonders. From the bustling streets of metropolitan areas to the serene beauty of national parks, every corner has its own unique charm. By staying mindful of safety and health, you'll not only protect yourself but also enhance your ability to fully immerse in the journey. Keeping a flexible attitude and being well-prepared ensures that even the unexpected becomes a cherished part of your adventure. Stay open to the spontaneity of travel, as those unplanned moments often leave the most lasting impressions.

CHAPTER 9

The Northeast region of the United States is a treasure trove of diverse landscapes, rich cultural history, and vibrant cities. For first-time travelers, the area offers a mix of modern city life and natural wonders, making it a compelling destination that requires some planning to truly appreciate. Whether you're drawn to the big-city energy of New York or the serenity of Acadia National Park, the Northeast delivers unique experiences that cater to every kind of traveler.

Arriving in the region is often easiest through major airports such as New York City's JFK or LaGuardia, Boston's Logan International, or Philadelphia International. Once you've touched down, the journey ahead depends on your itinerary. If you plan to explore the region's bustling cities, public transportation, such as the subway in New York City or the commuter rail in Boston, will be your best option. But for those hoping to get out and experience the scenic beauty of rural New England or the coastlines of Maine, renting a car is your best bet.

New York City is a fantastic starting point for a Northeast adventure. The city's many attractions are world-famous, and it's a place you can explore endlessly. Begin with Central Park, the green heart of the city. The park is vast, and there are countless ways to explore its beauty. You might enjoy walking or cycling its paths, or perhaps take a horse-drawn carriage ride through the wooded areas. After you've had your fill of nature, head down to Times Square for an iconic taste of the city's vibrancy. Even if you've seen it on screen, nothing compares to experiencing the lights and energy firsthand. From there, you can take a ferry from Battery Park to Liberty Island to view the Statue of Liberty up close—a must-do for anyone visiting the city. As you continue your journey through New York City, take the time to visit the 9/11 Memorial and Museum for a reflective experience that will deepen your understanding of a pivotal moment in U.S. history.

Beyond New York, there are countless scenic drives to experience. One of the region's top drives is the Kancamagus Highway in New Hampshire. This winding, 34-mile stretch through the White Mountains is particularly breathtaking in autumn when the foliage is at its peak. The vibrant oranges, reds, and yellows of the leaves will make you want to stop at every scenic overlook to snap a photo. Make sure to take your time and embrace the quiet, natural beauty that surrounds you. The Kancamagus Highway is a perfect place to pause and reflect, surrounded by the beauty of the New England wilderness.

Winter in the Northeast offers another kind of magic, particularly for those who love skiing. From Vermont's renowned Killington Resort to the mountains of New

Hampshire, the region offers a wide range of ski resorts. For beginners, most resorts offer lessons and gentle slopes, so you can enjoy the snow even if it's your first time on the skis. If you prefer a quieter experience, head to smaller resorts like those found in Maine, where the crowds are fewer and the atmosphere more relaxed.

If nature is your primary interest, Acadia National Park in Maine is one of the Northeast's crown jewels. The park, located along the rugged coast, is famous for its stunning vistas, diverse wildlife, and hiking trails. Whether you're hiking the Precipice Trail, walking along the carriage roads, or simply gazing out at the ocean from a mountaintop, Acadia offers a serene escape. During the summer months, the park comes alive with outdoor activities like boating, kayaking, and cycling, but fall is when it truly shines. The trees put on an incredible display of color, turning the park into a painter's palette of reds, oranges, and yellows. Winter transforms the park into a tranquil, snow-covered landscape perfect for cross-country skiing or snowshoeing.

Exploring small towns is another rewarding experience in the Northeast. Places like Bar Harbor in Maine or Stowe in Vermont embody the charm of rural New England. The slower pace of life in these towns provides an opportunity to connect with locals and enjoy the region's more laid-back side. You'll find farmers' markets, local art galleries, and cozy cafes perfect for lingering over a hot drink and chatting with the friendly locals. It's in these towns where you'll often hear the best stories, whether from a shop owner or a fisherman, giving you a deeper understanding of the area's culture.

The Hudson Valley in New York is another memorable stop on a Northeast tour. The rolling hills and charming villages offer a peaceful contrast to the busy city streets of New York City. The valley is a great place for wine lovers, with numerous vineyards offering tours and tastings. One of my favorite spots was the town of Hudson, with its beautiful antique shops and art galleries. Another highlight is the Walkway Over the Hudson, a pedestrian bridge that spans the river and provides one of the most picturesque views in the area.

As you venture through the Northeast, it's essential to remember that each season brings its own unique experience. Winters can be quite cold, particularly in the mountain regions, so be sure to dress in layers and bring warm clothes if you're planning outdoor activities. Spring and fall offer mild temperatures and are often the best times to visit for those who want to avoid the summer crowds while still enjoying pleasant weather. Summer can be busy, but it's also the time for hiking, boating, and exploring outdoor festivals, so it's a great option for adventure seekers.

However, beyond the breathtaking landscapes and outdoor activities, what truly makes the Northeast special is the people. Over the years, I've found that whether you're in a big city or a small town, the people in the Northeast are incredibly welcoming and proud of their history and culture. Striking up conversations with locals is one of the highlights of traveling through this region, as you'll often be given hidden gems to explore that you wouldn't find in any guidebook. Whether it's a friendly restaurant owner in Stowe or a park ranger in Acadia, the people are an integral part of the experience.

To truly enjoy your time in the Northeast, take it slow and savor the moments. The landscapes, people, and activities are all waiting for you, but it's the experience of immersing yourself in the local culture, chatting with the people, and taking the time to breathe in the atmosphere that will leave you with lasting memories. From the urban streets of New York City to the serene peaks of the White Mountains, the Northeast has something for everyone. Just remember to pack accordingly, depending on the season, and plan your days so you can experience everything this diverse region has to offer.

If you keep these tips in mind, you'll be able to navigate this stunning region with ease. No matter where your journey takes you, whether you're in a bustling city or a quiet rural town, the Northeast's charm, beauty, and hospitality will undoubtedly leave a lasting impression. So take your time, plan ahead, and allow yourself to experience this incredible corner of the United States in all its glory.

CHAPTER 10

When planning a journey through the South, it's essential to understand that this region isn't just about the destinations—it's about the stories and history woven into every corner of the land. If you're stepping into the South for the first time, you'll find that the charm lies in the depth of its culture, its rich historical roots, and the way it invites you to savor its landscapes, foods, and people. The region has a unique ability to make you feel like a part of something much larger than yourself, whether you're following the Civil Rights Trail or enjoying a leisurely drive along one of its coastal escapes. Each place has its own rhythm, and the experiences you gather will stay with you long after you've left.

Let's begin with one of the most significant routes in American history: the Civil Rights Trail. Spanning several states, this trail is a poignant reminder of the struggles, victories, and ongoing fight for equality. For a first-time visitor, starting in Birmingham, Alabama, is a good choice. The city was a hotbed for civil rights activity during the 1960s, and visiting the Birmingham Civil Rights Institute will give you an insightful look at the movement's history. From there, it's a short drive to Selma, where you can walk across the Edmund Pettus Bridge, site of the historic march for voting rights. Along the way, you'll find markers and museums that highlight the lives and sacrifices made for the cause, such as the National Civil Rights Museum in Memphis, Tennessee. This museum, housed in the Lorraine Motel (where Dr. Martin Luther King Jr. was assassinated), is a powerful experience that will make the history come alive in ways that words simply can't. The trail is filled with emotionally charged moments that invite you to reflect and understand the complexities of the civil rights movement.

Traveling from the Civil Rights Trail, you may want to change pace with a relaxing, scenic drive down the Natchez Trace Parkway. This historic route stretches from Mississippi to Tennessee, winding through forests, fields, and past small towns that seem to have been frozen in time. If you're interested in the deep history of the region, the Natchez Trace offers a glimpse into the path that Native Americans, European settlers, and pioneers once traveled. Start in Natchez, Mississippi, and make your way up to Nashville, Tennessee. Along the way, stop at landmarks like the Meriwether Lewis Monument, where the famed explorer died, or take a detour to the sunken remains of an old steamboat at the historical site of Jeff Busby Park. This drive offers a perfect mix of natural beauty and cultural significance.

While the inland routes are deeply historical, there's a certain allure to the South's coastal escapes. One of the most famous coastal regions is the Florida Keys. If you've ever dreamed of experiencing the laid-back island life, this is your place. You'll begin your journey in Miami, driving south along U.S. Highway 1. This drive, known as the Overseas Highway, will take you over numerous bridges that span the turquoise waters, leading you to each island paradise that comprises the Keys. A stop in Key Largo will allow you to enjoy diving or snorkeling in the crystal-clear waters, while Key West offers a more relaxed atmosphere with its charming streets lined with colorful homes and lively bars. As you continue south, make sure to visit the southernmost point of the continental U.S. in Key West, a symbol of the Keys' carefree spirit. Whether you're relaxing by the beach or exploring the local shops and cafes, the Florida Keys offer an unforgettable mix of sun, sea, and culture.

On the East Coast, the Outer Banks of North Carolina offer a different kind of coastal charm. This narrow string of barrier islands stretches along the state's coastline, and it's perfect for those looking to experience a blend of natural beauty and history. Begin in Kitty Hawk, where the Wright brothers made their historic first flight, and visit the Wright Brothers National Memorial to learn about their groundbreaking achievement. Then, take the scenic route along the Cape Hatteras National Seashore, stopping at its iconic lighthouse or strolling along its isolated beaches. As you travel along the Outer Banks, you'll also discover quaint villages like Ocracoke, where you can enjoy fresh seafood or rent a bike to explore the area's hidden corners. The Outer Banks are perfect for those who enjoy outdoor activities like kiteboarding or surfing, but if you prefer a quiet retreat, the secluded beaches offer a peaceful escape from the more crowded areas of the coast.

One of the most rewarding aspects of Southern travel is its food, and no journey through the South would be complete without a culinary road trip. The region is famed for its barbecue, bourbon, and so much more. One of the best places to experience a true Southern BBQ trail is in North Carolina, particularly along the eastern part of the state. The barbecue here is renowned for its vinegar-based sauces, which contrast with the sweeter styles found in other parts of the country. Start your journey in Raleigh, where you can try some of the best pulled pork sandwiches around. If you continue east, stop in towns like Goldsboro or Wilson, where local barbecue joints offer tender, slow-cooked meats that have been smoked to perfection. A visit to this part of the South will teach you that the barbecue is not just about food—it's about family traditions and a deep-rooted cultural experience.

As you move westward toward Kentucky, don't miss the opportunity to explore Bourbon Country. While bourbon distilleries are scattered across the state, the heart of bourbon country lies in the area between Lexington and Louisville. Start your tour at the famous Maker's Mark distillery in Loretto, where you can watch the process of making this iconic whiskey, and then continue on to the Woodford Reserve Distillery. Along the way, you'll pass rolling hills and lush farmland, where you can stop at charming towns that offer southern hospitality at its finest. The region's bourbon culture is intertwined with its agricultural history, and visiting these distilleries gives you a deep appreciation for the craft of whiskey-making.

While the journey through the South can take many different forms, one of the most memorable parts of it is the people you'll meet along the way. Southerners are proud of their history, their traditions, and their food, and they love sharing it with visitors. I've had countless conversations with locals who offered tips on the best places to eat or the most scenic spots to visit, and it's these personal interactions that make traveling through the South so rewarding. Whether you're chatting with a local farmer in Kentucky or a beach bartender in Key West, you'll find that the South's warmth and hospitality are among its most defining characteristics.

When traveling through the South, always be prepared for the region's weather. Summers can be hot and humid, so it's a good idea to dress in light, breathable clothing and drink plenty of water. If you're visiting the Gulf Coast or the Florida Keys, pack sunscreen and a hat to protect yourself from the intense sun. In winter, the weather is mild but can still get chilly in the evenings, so pack accordingly.

As you travel through the South, it's important to take your time and savor the journey. The region is rich in history, culture, and natural beauty, and there's always something new to discover around every corner. From the Civil Rights Trail to the beaches of the Outer Banks, from the culinary delights of North Carolina's barbecue to the tranquility of the Florida Keys, the South offers something for everyone. Embrace the slower pace, enjoy the hospitality of the locals, and don't rush—because the South is best experienced at a leisurely pace, with plenty of time to appreciate all it has to offer.

CHAPTER 11

Exploring the Midwest offers a unique experience for those looking to delve deep into America's heartland. The Midwest is often referred to as the "breadbasket of the nation," and rightfully so, with its vast landscapes of rural charm, rich history, and bustling cities that exude both nostalgia and modern vibrancy. Whether you're taking a leisurely drive along historic Route 66 or embarking on a lakeside retreat to places like Mackinac Island, the region provides something for every type of traveler, whether you're seeking adventure, relaxation, or cultural immersion.

Let's begin with Route 66, one of the most iconic roadways in the United States. Often dubbed "The Main Street of America," this route stretches from Chicago to Santa Monica, California, and offers a slice of

Americana unlike any other. Starting your journey in Chicago, the "Windy City," you'll quickly notice its vibrant energy and modern architecture. Before hitting the road, make sure to visit the Chicago History Museum, where you'll learn about the city's vital role in the development of Route 66. It's an ideal way to grasp the historical significance of the route before you embark on your own journey.

Once you leave Chicago behind, the transition from urban sprawl to open, expansive fields is striking. As you make your way to Pontiac, Illinois, a quaint town that celebrates Route 66, take the time to explore the Route 66 Hall of Fame Museum. This small but fascinating museum showcases historical relics like vintage automobiles and neon signs, offering a glimpse into the past when Route 66 was a symbol of freedom and exploration.

Further south, you'll reach St. Louis, Missouri, a city known for the iconic

Gateway Arch. Standing tall at 630 feet, the Arch is the tallest monument in the U.S. and offers a breathtaking view of the Mississippi River and the surrounding cityscape. While in St. Louis, take a moment to explore its vibrant culture, including the famous Soulard neighborhood, home to lively pubs and historic buildings.

As you continue your journey down Route 66, stop in Springfield, Missouri, where you can experience some of the nostalgic roadside motels, diners, and classic Americana. Towns along the way offer unique insights into the past, where you can enjoy local food, quirky roadside attractions, and fascinating museums that celebrate the culture and history of this famed route.

A truly remarkable drive is the Great River Road, which stretches alongside the Mississippi River, offering some of the most scenic landscapes in the Midwest. This route will lead you through towns like Galena, Illinois, where you can explore 19th-century architecture, cobblestone streets, and antique shops. Galena, rich in Civil War history, offers both a picturesque experience and historical insight, perfect for anyone looking to step back in time.

From Illinois, as you follow the river south, you'l eventually find yourself crossing into Wisconsin, where the landscape begins to shift into rolling hills and lush forests. The town of La Crosse, situated along the banks of the Mississippi River, is known for its stunning views, especially in autumn, when the leaves transform into vibrant hues of red, orange, and yellow. La Crosse is also home to several breweries, where you can sample the region's best beers and enjoy live music in a relaxed setting.

If you crave a closer connection with nature, the Great Lakes region is where you'll want to be. The five Great Lakes—Superior, Michigan, Huron, Erie, and Ontario—are not only the largest freshwater lakes in the world but also offer a wealth of activities.

Begin your exploration with a trip to Mackinac Island, Michigan. To reach the island, hop on a ferry from the mainland, and you'll soon find yourself in a place where cars are banned, and transportation is done by horse-drawn carriage or bicycle. This offers a peaceful and unique escape from the bustle of everyday life.

Mackinac Island is famous for its fudge, and as you explore, be sure to visit one of the many shops selling this sweet treat. The island is also home to historical sites like Fort Mackinac, a well-preserved military post offering historical reenactments and exhibits that transport you to the 18th century. As you explore the island's scenic trails or ride a bike around the perimeter, you'll be treated to views of the surrounding waters of Lake Huron, a perfect spot for photography.

Continuing along Lake Michigan, the city of Chicago provides plenty of opportunities for exploration. From the magnificent Navy

Pier, you can ride the Ferris wheel to get a panoramic view of the lake and the skyline. Chicago is also home to world-class museums, including the Art Institute of Chicago, and a vibrant food scene. Be sure to grab a slice of deep-dish pizza, a Chicago classic, before leaving.

Head north to Duluth, Minnesota, for another lakeside experience. This charming town on the shores of Lake Superior offers a mix of rugged natural beauty and outdoor adventure. Whether hiking the trails that wind through the forest or simply strolling along the waterfront, Duluth offers something for everyone. In the winter, it transforms into a snow-covered wonderland, perfect for winter sports such as skiing and ice fishing.

For a more tranquil escape, Door County, Wisconsin, is the place to be. Known for its stunning coastline along Lake Michigan, Door County is a peaceful destination filled with charming small towns like Fish Creek and Egg Harbor. Explore the Door County Coastal Byway, which offers scenic views and access to secluded beaches. The area is also famous for its wineries, making it a perfect destination for wine lovers. Kayaking, hiking, and exploring lighthouses are all popular activities here, giving visitors plenty of ways to enjoy the natural beauty.

As we venture into the heartland, one of the unique aspects of the Midwest is its rural charm. It's a region defined by wide-open spaces, farming communities, and county fairs. A quintessential experience is attending a state fair, such as the Illinois State Fair in Springfield, where you can see everything from livestock exhibitions to exciting rides and live entertainment. These fairs give you an authentic taste of rural life, complete with homemade pies, cotton candy, and local crafts.

Beyond the fairs, the rural Midwest is filled with picturesque towns and communities. The Amish country in Iowa, for example, offers an entirely different pace of life. In towns like Jamesport, you'll see horse-drawn buggies instead of cars and can purchase homemade goods like quilts, baked goods, and jams from local shops. This tranquil area is perfect for anyone looking to escape the fast-paced city life and immerse themselves in simpler times.

The Midwest is also home to a variety of festivals and events throughout the year. From apple picking in Michigan's orchards to the tulip festival in Holland, Michigan, there's always something to celebrate. These events provide opportunities to experience local traditions and enjoy the best of regional cuisine, from farm-to-table dining to street food that's served at festivals.

When traveling through the Midwest, renting a car is often the best way to explore the area. Public transportation is limited in rural areas, and having a car allows you to fully immerse yourself in the region's small towns, scenic byways, and attractions. Be sure to plan your route ahead of time, particularly if you are venturing into more remote areas, where gas stations and food stops can be few and far between.

The Midwest also offers a range of accommodations, from charming bed-and-breakfasts and historic inns to modern hotels in bustling cities. If you're traveling along Route 66, staying at one of the old-fashioned motels along the route is a great way to embrace the nostalgia of the road. These motels, often adorned with neon signs, provide a glimpse into the past while offering modern comforts.

In terms of food, the Midwest excels in comfort food. From hearty steaks in Kansas City to the famous Chicago-style hot dogs and deep-dish pizza, the region is known for its flavorful and filling cuisine. Be sure to try regional specialties like cheese curds in Wisconsin, pork tenderloin sandwiches in Indiana, and apple pie in Michigan. Each state offers its own take on classic American dishes, providing travelers with delicious experiences to savor.

The beauty of the Midwest lies in its diversity. Whether you're cruising down Route 66, enjoying the lakeside landscapes, or immersing yourself in rural Americana, each destination offers something unique. From the energy of Chicago to the quiet charm of small towns, the Midwest captures the essence of American culture. The region's landscapes, history, and people create an unforgettable travel experience that will leave you with lasting memories. It's not just about the places you visit, but the journey itself—the open roads, the scenic vistas, and the warm hospitality that make the Midwest truly special.

CHAPTER 12

Exploring the Western United States presents an adventure like no other, offering travelers a variety of landscapes ranging from expansive deserts to towering mountains and lush valleys. This region provides some of the most iconic scenic routes, renowned national parks, and world-class wine regions, each waiting to be discovered. Whether you are cruising down the Pacific Coast Highway, hiking through Yosemite's granite cliffs, or savoring a glass of wine in Oregon's Willamette Valley, the West is a treasure trove of natural beauty and diverse experiences. For first-time visitors, navigating this vast and varied region can feel overwhelming, but with a bit of guidance, you can fully immerse yourself in its wonders, whether you're seeking rugged adventure, serene relaxation, or cultural enrichment.

Start your journey along one of the most legendary roads in the U.S.—the Pacific Coast Highway. This stretch of coastal road offers spectacular views, weaving through some of the most picturesque landscapes in the country. As you begin in Southern California, from Los Angeles or Santa Monica, you'll experience the blend of coastal charm and urban sophistication before you make your way north. The Pacific Coast Highway guides you past serene beaches, seaside cliffs, and charming beach towns. In Malibu, you can take a moment to relax on the sand or explore the scenic vistas along the coast. As you continue further up the road, you'll enter Big Sur, where the dramatic cliffs meet the Pacific Ocean, creating one of the most awe-inspiring views in the world. Big Sur is home to some of the best-known landmarks, such as Bixby Creek Bridge, where you can stop and take in the sweeping views.

Continuing further north, the small town of Carmel-by-the-Sea offers a quaint retreat with galleries and shops, while Monterey is perfect for those wanting to explore its rich maritime history, especially the famous Monterey Bay Aquarium.

The next section of the Pacific Coast Highway takes you through the beautiful coastal region of Northern California. As you make your way toward San Francisco, you'll pass through the coastal town of Santa Cruz, known for its laid-back vibe and famous boardwalk. Once you arrive in San Francisco, you'll find a city steeped in history and full of exciting things to do. No visit is complete without seeing the Golden Gate Bridge, but be sure to venture into neighborhoods like the Mission District for its colorful murals, or take a walk through Golden Gate Park for an afternoon of peaceful exploration. Afterward, a visit to Alcatraz Island is highly recommended—its fascinating history as a former prison is enhanced by the captivating views of the bay. Once you've had your fill of the city, it's time to transition from the bustle of the city to the tranquility of wine country.

California's Napa and Sonoma Valleys offer the perfect escape from urban life. Known worldwide for their vineyards, these regions are a wine lover's paradise, offering both fine dining and scenic beauty. Begin your wine country adventure in Napa, where you can tour renowned wineries such as Robert Mondavi and Castello di Amorosa. The peaceful atmosphere of Napa Valley is perfect for leisurely vineyard tours, whether by bicycle, on foot, or even by hot air balloon, which gives you an incredible bird's-eye view of the rolling hills covered with grapevines. If you prefer a more intimate experience, Sonoma offers a more relaxed pace with smaller, boutique wineries where you can chat with local winemakers and sample exquisite wines. Don't forget to indulge in the region's famous farm-to-table cuisine, where fresh ingredients complement the wines perfectly. Sonoma's town square is also a charming place to explore, with local shops, galleries, and cafés creating a welcoming, laid-back atmosphere.

As you make your way eastward, the national parks of the West will leave you in awe of their majestic beauty. Yosemite National Park is one of the most iconic parks in the United States, known for its towering granite cliffs, lush meadows, and ancient sequoia trees. The park's centerpiece, Yosemite Valley, is where you'll find famous landmarks like El Capitan, Half Dome, and Bridalveil Fall. Hiking is one of the best ways to experience the park, with trails like the moderate Mist Trail or the more challenging Half Dome hike offering an up-close experience of the park's natural splendor. For an unforgettable experience, take the Glacier Point Trail, which offers sweeping views of the valley and the surrounding wilderness. Yosemite is not just a park for hikers; it's a place for everyone to connect with nature, whether you're camping under the stars, enjoying a peaceful picnic by the Merced River, or marveling at the breathtaking views.

Another bucket-list destination in the West is Yellowstone National Park, the first national park in the world. Located primarily in Wyoming, Yellowstone is famous for its geothermal wonders, including hot springs, geysers, and colorful mineral pools. The park is home to incredible wildlife, and you're likely to see bison, elk, and possibly even a grizzly bear. One of the park's main attractions is Old Faithful, the geyser that erupts approximately every 90 minutes. Be sure to also visit the Grand Prismatic Spring, whose brilliant blue, green, and orange hues make it one of the most photographed locations in the park. Yellowstone offers a variety of activities, from hiking and fishing to taking scenic drives, allowing visitors to enjoy the park's beauty at their own pace.

If you're seeking a more iconic desert landscape, the Grand Canyon National Park in Arizona is a must-see. The immense scale of the Grand Canyon, carved over millions of years by the Colorado River, is impossible to fully comprehend until you witness it in person. The views from the South Rim are spectacular, and you can explore the area through various hiking trails, from easy walks to challenging descents down into the canyon itself. For a truly unique experience, consider booking a helicopter tour to see the canyon from the air—an experience that provides an entirely new perspective on this natural wonder. Whether you're standing on the edge of the canyon, hiking its trails, or rafting in the Colorado River, the Grand Canyon will undoubtedly leave you in awe of nature's power.

Beyond the national parks, the West is also home to some exceptional wine regions. In addition to California's Napa and Sonoma, Oregon's Willamette Valley is rapidly gaining recognition for its fine Pinot Noir wines. Situated just south of Portland, the valley offers a more laid-back alternative to California's wine regions, where you can enjoy the rolling hills and lush vineyards. The cooler climate of the Willamette Valley gives the region's wines a distinct flavor profile, and many wineries offer tastings in intimate settings, providing visitors with the chance to meet the winemakers and learn about the local terroir.

Whether you're driving along the Pacific Coast Highway, exploring iconic national parks like Yosemite and Yellowstone, or sipping wine in one of the country's best wine regions, the West is a place that offers a lifetime of adventures. This region is filled with diverse landscapes, each telling its own story and providing visitors with the opportunity to reconnect with nature, immerse themselves in culture, and create unforgettable memories. Along the way, don't forget to interact with the locals—whether they are guiding you through a vineyard, sharing their knowledge of the national parks, or offering a recommendation for a hidden gem of a town to visit, their insights will add a personal touch to your journey. With each mile, you'll discover why the West continues to be one of the most cherished travel destinations in the world.

CHAPTER 13

Finding the perfect place to stay during your travels is a crucial step that sets the tone for your entire journey. Whether you're exploring a bustling city, relaxing by the seaside, or venturing into the wilderness, the right accommodation enhances your experience. From luxury hotels to quirky unique stays, every option carries its charm, and making an informed choice ensures a memorable trip.

When arriving in an unfamiliar city, especially as a first-time visitor, choosing a place to stay can feel overwhelming. A good starting point is to consider what you value most—whether it's proximity to attractions, access to nature, affordability, or a unique experience that reflects the local culture. Understanding the layout of the city or region is vital. Central locations often provide convenience for exploring landmarks and restaurants, while quieter neighborhoods offer a more relaxed, immersive experience.

Hotels are the go-to choice for many travelers because they cater to a wide range of needs and budgets. Luxury establishments with their rooftop pools, wellness spas, and fine dining attract those looking to indulge. At the same time, mid-range hotels deliver comfort without breaking the bank, often including practical amenities such as complimentary breakfasts or shuttle services to nearby attractions. Budget travelers, too, can find excellent value in affordable chains or independently run hotels that focus on essentials like clean rooms, good service, and strategic locations. When selecting a hotel, always consider its proximity to key places you plan to visit and assess features like Wi-Fi access, parking, and late check-in options to match your itinerary.

Motels and inns offer an alternative for travelers who appreciate simplicity, often located along highways or in smaller towns. Ideal for road-trippers or those seeking to avoid the bustle of urban centers, motels provide convenient parking and a welcoming atmosphere. Inns, on the other hand, add a touch of charm, frequently run by locals eager to share insider tips on what to see and do in the area. These accommodations might lack the luxury of larger hotels, but their personalized touches—such as homemade breakfasts or intimate common areas—often leave a lasting impression.

For those drawn to nature, campgrounds and RV parks provide an opportunity to sleep under the stars and immerse yourself in the great outdoors. Whether you prefer pitching a tent by a serene lake or parking an RV in a forested area, these spots offer a refreshing break from city life. Many campgrounds come equipped with basic amenities such as bathrooms, picnic areas, and even Wi-Fi, balancing adventure with comfort. Planning is key to enjoying this experience—be sure to pack weather-appropriate gear, familiarize yourself with local wildlife, and understand the rules of the park to ensure a safe and enjoyable stay.

In recent years, unique accommodations have gained popularity among travelers seeking something extraordinary. Glamping, or glamorous camping, combines the rustic appeal of camping with the comfort of high-end amenities. Imagine staying in a spacious, beautifully furnished tent complete with a king-sized bed, electricity, and even a private bathroom. Similarly, treehouses, converted barns, or historic lodges offer distinctive experiences that go beyond traditional stays. Staying in such places not only enriches your trip but also provides stories to share long after your return home.

Booking the right accommodation involves more than just selecting a place to sleep; it's about finding a base that complements your travel style. Begin by identifying your priorities—whether they're related to convenience, budget, or experience—and use this to narrow your options. Online booking platforms can help you compare prices and read reviews, but don't overlook the value of contacting accommodations directly for personalized advice or potential discounts.

Practical considerations also play an important role. If you're arriving early or leaving late, confirm whether the property can store your luggage to make transitions smoother. Travelers with cars should check parking availability and costs, while international visitors might want to verify language support or currency exchange services. For families, accommodations offering amenities like kitchenettes or separate sleeping areas can simplify daily routines, while solo adventurers may prefer social settings such as hostels to meet like-minded travelers.

Reflecting on personal experiences can add depth to your decision-making process. Staying at a rustic inn once provided an opportunity to connect with the locals, whose recommendations for hidden trails and family-owned restaurants made the trip unforgettable. Another time, waking up in a luxury glamping tent to a sunrise over rolling hills created a sense of serenity unmatched by any hotel. These moments highlight how the right accommodation can elevate your trip from ordinary to exceptional.

Conversations with locals often reveal insights you won't find in guidebooks. A friendly bartender might recommend a budget-friendly motel with stunning views, while a taxi driver could point out an off-the-beaten-path bed-and-breakfast known for its hospitality. These interactions not only enhance your stay but also deepen your connection to the destination.

For travelers who like to plan meticulously, a few practical tips can help. Always read reviews critically, looking for details that align with your priorities. For instance, a quiet traveler may value soundproof rooms, while a foodie might seek accommodations near vibrant dining areas. Consider the timing of your booking—many places offer discounts for reservations made well in advance, while others provide last-minute deals for spontaneous trips. Packing smartly can also make a difference, especially if you plan to stay in unique or rural accommodations where amenities might differ from urban hotels.

Choosing the right place to stay can significantly shape your travel memories. By thoughtfully balancing comfort, convenience, and a sense of adventure, you can find accommodations that don't just meet your needs but enhance your journey. Whether you're enjoying the luxury of a five-star hotel, the coziness of a family-run inn, the freedom of a campsite, or the novelty of a unique stay, every choice offers a new perspective on the world. Planning carefully and embracing the unexpected ensures your accommodations are more than just a place to sleep—they become an integral part of your travel story.

CHAPTER 14

Embarking on a journey across the United States is a feast for the senses, and one of the most rewarding aspects of traveling is discovering the diverse culinary delights scattered across the country. Deciding where to eat while on the road can be an adventure in itself, leading you to unexpected gems that satisfy your hunger and create unforgettable memories. From classic roadside diners steeped in nostalgia to the innovative flavors served from vibrant food trucks, the options are as boundless as the horizons you'll encounter.

Roadside diners hold a special place in American travel culture, often serving as an oasis for weary travelers seeking comfort and familiarity. These establishments, frequently nestled along highways or near scenic byways, evoke a sense of timeless charm. The moment you step inside, you're greeted by the aroma of freshly brewed coffee and sizzling bacon. Decorated with retro booths, neon signs, and friendly faces behind the counter, diners offer an inviting atmosphere. The menus are typically vast, catering to every craving, whether it's a hearty breakfast plate, a juicy burger with a side of crispy fries, or a towering slice of homemade pie. These diners are more than just a place to eat; they are a slice of Americana, offering an authentic glimpse into the lives and traditions of the locals.

Food trucks, by contrast, bring a contemporary twist to the roadside dining experience. These mobile kitchens, often painted in bold, eye-catching designs, serve up dishes that are as creative as they are delicious. The beauty of food trucks lies in their ability to capture the essence of a region's culinary heritage while infusing it with modern innovation. Imagine savoring fish tacos drizzled with spicy lime crema along California's coast or devouring a plate of pulled pork sliders in the heart of the

Carolinas. Tracking down food trucks can add a sense of adventure to your trip, as many post their ever-changing locations on social media. This allows you to experience the thrill of the hunt, knowing that the reward is a meal made with passion and creativity.

The culinary landscape of the United States is a patchwork of regional specialties, each state offering its own unique flavors. Sampling these iconic dishes is like taking a journey through the nation's history and culture. In the Southwest, you'll find bold, spicy dishes like green chile stew and Navajo tacos, reflecting the area's rich Native American and Mexican influences. The Midwest, known for its comfort food, invites you to try cheese curds, butter burgers, and gooey hotdish casseroles. Head to the Pacific Northwest, and you'll encounter an abundance of fresh seafood, from Dungeness crab to smoked salmon, paired with local wines and craft beers. In the Deep South, dishes like shrimp and grits, fried green tomatoes, and pecan pie tell the story of a region steeped in tradition and hospitality. Every state offers its own edible treasures, waiting to be discovered by curious travelers.

For those traveling on a budget, dining on the road doesn't have to break the bank. Affordable and delicious options are plentiful if you know where to look. Local diners, which often serve hearty meals at reasonable prices, are a great starting point. Grocery stores and farmers' markets are another resourceful choice, providing everything from freshly baked bread and local cheeses to ready-to-eat meals that allow you to enjoy a picnic in a scenic location. Chain restaurants, while less adventurous, can offer consistency and familiarity, especially if you're traveling with children or have dietary restrictions. Planning ahead and setting aside a portion of your budget specifically for food ensures you can indulge in memorable meals without overspending.

Eating on the road also provides an opportunity to connect with locals, who are often eager to share their favorite hidden gems. A quick chat with a gas station attendant or a barista can lead you to the best barbecue joint in town or a food truck serving the fluffiest beignets. These personal recommendations often take you off the beaten path, allowing you to explore neighborhoods and towns that you might otherwise have overlooked.

Personal experiences often highlight the magic of roadside dining. During one cross-country trip, a stop at a small-town diner led to a conversation with the owner, who shared the history of their secret pie recipe. Another memorable meal came from a food truck parked on a sunny pier, where the chef handed out samples of his signature crab cakes while sharing stories about his fishing adventures. These moments turn meals into memories, making the journey as satisfying as the destination.

Practical considerations are key to enjoying your culinary adventures. Before hitting the road, research the local specialties of your destination to create a "must-try" list. Apps and websites can help you locate highly rated eateries, but don't hesitate to rely on word-of-mouth tips from locals. Be mindful of operating hours, as many family-run diners and food trucks may close early or only operate during specific days of the week. If you're traveling with a group, discussing preferences and dietary needs in advance can save time and ensure everyone enjoys the experience.

One of the joys of exploring the United States is discovering that food is not just sustenance but an integral part of the journey. From the nostalgic charm of roadside diners to the culinary creativity of food trucks and the rich history embedded in regional dishes, every meal adds a new layer to your travel story. By staying open to new experiences, asking locals for recommendations, and embracing the unexpected, you'll not only nourish your body but also feed your soul, creating memories that will linger long after the last bite.

CHAPTER 15

Planning activities and entertainment while exploring the United States opens up an abundance of opportunities, catering to both thrill-seekers and those who prefer a slower pace. The sheer variety of experiences available ensures that every traveler, regardless of their interests, will find something to captivate their imagination. From discovering scenic hiking trails to relaxing on pristine beaches, the choices are as diverse as the country's landscapes. Tailoring your journey to include outdoor adventures, engaging cultural experiences, and moments of awe in nature guarantees a memorable and fulfilling trip.

Exploring the outdoors often serves as the highlight of any adventure. Imagine yourself stepping onto a quiet forest trail, the sound of leaves crunching underfoot as sunlight filters through the canopy above. Hiking is one of the most accessible ways to experience nature's splendor, with trails ranging from easy strolls to rigorous climbs that reward you with panoramic views. On one such trek, I recall cresting a hill to see an endless expanse of rolling green mountains, a moment of pure serenity that made the effort entirely worthwhile. For those new to hiking, starting with shorter, well-marked paths is a good way to build confidence while soaking in the surroundings.

Cycling offers a dynamic way to explore the countryside or urban areas, providing a mix of exercise and sightseeing. Many towns and cities boast bike-friendly routes, often winding through parks, past historic landmarks, or along waterfronts. Renting a bike locally can save the hassle of bringing your own and often includes guided tours or maps of the best paths. Whether you're coasting down a serene coastal trail or navigating the energetic streets of a bustling city, biking immerses you in your surroundings in a way few other activities can.

Water-based activities also bring their own charm. Kayaking allows travelers to glide along tranquil waters, whether it's a placid lake surrounded by lush greenery or a meandering river with gentle bends. One unforgettable experience involved paddling into a hidden cove where the water was so clear it seemed like floating on air. For those looking for an adrenaline rush, rafting down whitewater rapids provides a thrilling challenge, combining teamwork and excitement. Whatever your choice, safety is paramount—always wear a life jacket and follow your guide's instructions carefully.

Beaches hold a universal appeal, offering everything from peaceful relaxation to lively water sports. The U.S. coastline stretches thousands of miles, each region presenting its own unique flavor. Whether you're lounging under an umbrella with a good book, collecting seashells along the shore, or diving into the waves, beach days create memories filled with sun, laughter, and serenity. For more adventurous travelers, activities like jet skiing, parasailing, or snorkeling add excitement, revealing underwater worlds brimming with vibrant marine life. Checking local rental shops or guided tours can make these activities accessible to even first-timers.

For wildlife enthusiasts, national parks and reserves offer unparalleled opportunities to observe animals in their natural habitats. Picture yourself in a quiet meadow, binoculars in hand, watching a herd of elk graze at dawn or an eagle soar gracefully overhead. Each park is unique in its offerings—some are renowned for large mammals like bears and bison, while others are havens for birdwatchers or marine life enthusiasts. Visiting during less crowded hours, such as early mornings or weekdays, often increases your chances of spotting animals and enhances the sense of immersion.

National parks also serve as gateways to some of the most breathtaking landscapes in the world. The towering rock formations of Arches National Park, the vibrant geothermal pools of Yellowstone, and the endless depths of the Grand Canyon are just a few examples of the wonders awaiting exploration. These parks often offer ranger-led programs, providing deeper insights into the area's history, geology, and ecology. If you're traveling with children, many parks also have junior ranger programs, turning the visit into an educational adventure for the whole family.

Conversations with locals can reveal hidden treasures and elevate your trip. During one visit to a small coastal town, a local shop owner pointed me toward a secluded hiking trail that led to a cliffside vantage point with breathtaking ocean views. Such insider knowledge often leads to experiences that are off the beaten path, offering a sense of discovery that adds depth to your journey. Similarly, chatting with a park ranger or guide often yields tips on lesser-known trails or the best times to visit popular spots to avoid crowds.

Practical planning goes a long way in ensuring your adventures are enjoyable. Always check the weather forecast and dress accordingly, layering clothing if temperatures fluctuate. Comfortable footwear is a must for hiking or exploring uneven terrain, and carrying a small daypack with essentials like water, snacks, sunscreen, and a map ensures you're prepared for any eventuality. If you're planning to participate in guided activities like rafting or wildlife tours, booking in advance is advisable, particularly during peak travel seasons when availability can be limited.

Traveling sustainably is also important when enjoying the outdoors. Respecting natural habitats, staying on designated paths, and minimizing waste are all simple ways to preserve the beauty of these places for future generations. Bring a reusable water bottle and bags to reduce single-use plastic, and follow any guidelines set by local authorities or park staff to protect the environment.

As you explore the wide array of activities and entertainment options available in the United States, you'll find that the experiences go beyond what you see—they touch what you feel. From the exhilaration of scaling a challenging trail to the peacefulness of watching a sunset over a quiet bay, these moments create connections to the places you visit and the people you meet. By embracing the unexpected, staying curious, and taking time to truly immerse yourself in each experience, you'll leave with memories that are as vivid as the landscapes themselves. The journey becomes more than just a series of destinations; it transforms into a story of adventure, growth, and discovery that you'll treasure forever.

CHAPTER 16

When the sun dips below the horizon, the United States transforms into a vibrant landscape of nighttime activities and entertainment. Each region offers its own take on how to enjoy the hours after dark, from bustling live music venues to serene stargazing spots. Whether you're seeking the buzz of city nightlife, the intimacy of a quiet bar, or a one-of-a-kind nighttime adventure, there's no shortage of options to explore. For first-time visitors, diving into a city's nightlife is a way to connect with its culture, energy, and people, creating experiences that linger long after the night ends.

Live music is often the heartbeat of any city's evening scene. Across the country, music venues come alive with a mix of local talent and world-renowned artists. Stepping into a historic venue, you're immediately enveloped by the sound of guitars strumming, drums beating, and voices filling the space with melody. In cities like

Memphis, where the roots of blues and soul run deep, the energy is palpable. Walking into a club on Beale Street, you might find yourself swaying to live blues, the raw emotion in the music echoing the soul of the city. In Austin, Texas, live music spills from nearly every corner, with genres ranging from indie rock to country, ensuring there's something for every taste.

For those who enjoy a more laid-back vibe, small jazz clubs and acoustic sets provide an intimate setting to unwind. In places like New Orleans, jazz isn't just music—it's a way of life. You can spend an evening in a dimly lit bar, sipping on a cocktail while a saxophone croons in the background, the atmosphere charged with history and culture. These venues often feel like hidden gems, offering an authentic slice of the city's musical heritage.

Bars and clubs across the United States add another layer to the nightlife experience. Each city has its own unique approach to nightlife, reflecting its personality and culture. In Los Angeles, trendy rooftop bars offer panoramic views of the city skyline, paired with innovative drinks and a glamorous atmosphere. Meanwhile, in Miami, the nightlife is all about energy, with clubs pulsing to the beat of Latin music until the early hours of the morning. For a more understated evening, speakeasies in Chicago or San Francisco provide a nostalgic twist, combining expertly crafted cocktails with a touch of mystery and exclusivity.

For travelers who prefer something off the beaten path, nighttime activities can take on a whole new meaning. Stargazing is a mesmerizing way to connect with nature and the universe. In remote areas like Utah's Arches National Park or California's Joshua Tree, the lack of light pollution reveals a star-filled sky that feels infinite. Lying on your back, tracing constellations, and watching for shooting stars creates a sense of peace and wonder that's hard to find in the busyness of everyday life. On one memorable night, I joined a guided stargazing tour in a dark-sky reserve, where the guide used a laser pointer to outline constellations and shared captivating stories about their origins. The experience was as enlightening as it was awe-inspiring.

If you're seeking more active nighttime adventures, options abound. Moonlit kayaking trips offer a serene yet exhilarating way to explore waterways, with the glow of the moon casting a silvery light on the water's surface. Guided night hikes provide a chance to witness nocturnal wildlife, hear the rustle of leaves in the dark, and experience nature from a completely different perspective. Urban evening bike tours, on the other hand, allow you to see a city in a new light, with illuminated landmarks and quiet streets creating a magical atmosphere.

Personal stories often highlight the magic of nightlife. On one occasion in Seattle, I followed a local's recommendation to a small, hidden bar that featured live acoustic performances. The atmosphere was electric, the music soulful, and the conversations with locals unforgettable. Another time, during a visit to Sedona, Arizona, I found myself on a hilltop stargazing tour. The guide handed out telescopes and shared insights about the night sky, making the experience both educational and deeply moving.

Connecting with locals is one of the best ways to uncover the unique aspects of a destination's nightlife. A quick conversation with a bartender might lead you to an unassuming venue that serves the best craft cocktails in town, or a chat with a fellow concert-goer might introduce you to an up-and-coming band you'll soon be adding to your playlist. Locals often have their finger on the pulse of what's happening, offering tips and insights that elevate your experience from touristy to truly authentic.

Practical planning can ensure you make the most of your evenings. Researching events and venues ahead of time helps you prioritize what to do, whether it's attending a sold-out concert or joining a guided nighttime tour. Checking dress codes, especially for upscale bars or clubs, ensures you're prepared, while booking tickets or reservations early secures your spot at popular attractions. Staying aware of your surroundings, particularly in busy nightlife areas, and arranging reliable transportation, such as rideshares or designated drivers, helps ensure a safe and enjoyable night.

Nightlife is about more than just entertainment—it's a chance to immerse yourself in the spirit of a place. Every city, town, and region has its own interpretation of how to celebrate after the sun sets, whether through the rhythm of live music, the camaraderie of a lively bar, or the serenity of a quiet moment under the stars. By embracing these opportunities, asking for local recommendations, and keeping an open mind, you'll discover a side of travel that's vibrant, memorable, and uniquely yours. These nighttime adventures become an integral part of your journey, adding depth, excitement, and a touch of magic to your travel story.

CHAPTER 17

Traveling across the United States offers countless opportunities to shop for unique items and discover the rich cultural tapestry of each region. Whether you're exploring bustling urban centers, charming small towns, or scenic countryside markets, shopping is a chance to connect with the local spirit and take home meaningful souvenirs. For first-time visitors, finding the perfect items can feel like a treasure hunt, and with a little planning, the journey becomes as rewarding as the purchases themselves.

One of the most delightful ways to shop in the United States is by visiting local markets and artisan fairs. These vibrant spaces often feature skilled craftspeople displaying their handmade goods, which range from jewelry and pottery to woven textiles and carved wood pieces. Each item carries a story, reflecting the traditions and creativity of the maker. Imagine strolling through a market in the Southwest, where intricate silver and turquoise jewelry catches the sunlight, or visiting a New England coastal town and finding hand-knitted sweaters that evoke the warmth of the region's maritime heritage. These markets not only offer unique items but also provide an opportunity to meet the artisans, hear their stories, and learn about the techniques that make their work special.

Modern shopping enthusiasts can find their paradise at outlet malls scattered across the country. These expansive centers combine high-end brands and discounted prices, making them a popular destination for travelers looking for deals. Whether it's a luxury handbag at a fraction of its original price or a pair of comfortable walking shoes for the rest of your journey, outlet malls cater to a variety of needs and budgets. During one visit to a sprawling outlet mall in Pennsylvania, I discovered a store specializing in outdoor gear, which proved invaluable for the hiking trails I planned to explore later in my trip. The key to maximizing your time at outlet malls is to plan your visit carefully, prioritize the stores you're most interested in, and keep an eye out for seasonal sales that offer even greater savings.

Antique shops are a treasure trove for those who appreciate history and character. These charming stores, often filled with a mix of vintage furniture, collectibles, and one-of-a-kind trinkets, invite you to browse at your own pace and uncover hidden gems. Walking into an antique shop feels like stepping into a different era, where each item holds a piece of the past waiting to be rediscovered. On one memorable visit to an antique store in the Midwest, I stumbled upon a beautifully preserved quilt that told a story of craftsmanship and care, becoming a cherished reminder of my travels. Antique hunting requires patience and an eye for detail, but the rewards often far exceed the effort.

Conversations with locals can lead to surprising discoveries and enrich your shopping experience. A friendly chat with a shopkeeper might reveal a nearby boutique selling handmade candles, or a recommendation from a local resident could guide you to a family-run gallery featuring works by regional artists. During one trip to the Pacific Northwest, a barista suggested a small bookstore tucked away on a quiet street, where I found rare prints of maps showcasing the area's natural beauty. These personal interactions not only lead to unique finds but also deepen your connection to the community.

Practical tips can make your shopping adventures more enjoyable and efficient. Researching ahead of time is crucial, especially if you're visiting during a festival or special event where markets may be busier than usual. Carrying cash is helpful when visiting local markets or antique shops, as smaller vendors may not accept cards. Bringing a reusable bag ensures you have a convenient way to carry your purchases while reducing waste. If you're shopping for fragile or heavy items, consider shipping them home to avoid complications during your travels.

When choosing souvenirs, think about items that hold personal significance or reflect the culture of the region you're visiting. Instead of standard tourist trinkets, look for items like locally made soaps, gourmet treats, or handcrafted decor. In California, a bottle of wine from a family-owned vineyard makes a meaningful gift, while in Louisiana, a jar of homemade Creole spice mix brings a taste of the region's cuisine to your kitchen. By selecting souvenirs that tell a story or evoke a memory, you're creating connections that last far beyond the trip itself.

The timing of your shopping excursions can also influence your experience. Arriving early at markets ensures a better selection and fewer crowds, while exploring antique shops on weekdays often provides a quieter atmosphere for browsing. For outlet malls, visiting during midweek or off-peak hours allows you to shop more comfortably and take advantage of the best deals without the rush.

Shopping isn't just about acquiring items— it's an opportunity to immerse yourself in the local culture, interact with the people who bring their creativity to life, and bring home pieces that serve as reminders of your journey. Whether you're exploring vibrant artisan markets, hunting for bargains at outlet malls, or uncovering treasures in antique stores, each experience adds a new layer of richness to your travels. By keeping an open mind, engaging with locals, and exploring thoughtfully, you'll discover that shopping can be as much about the adventure as it is about the souvenirs you take home.

CHAPTER 18

To see all the details and track your package, simply scan the code below. It's super easy and will give you all the information you need to know about your delivery!!!!!

Embarking on a road trip across the United States is an adventure filled with freedom and the thrill of exploration. Each mile promises new scenery, unique attractions, and the chance to experience life on the road. However, the success of such a journey lies in careful preparation, an adaptable mindset, and practical strategies for handling everything from everyday inconveniences to unexpected emergencies. Whether you're traveling solo, with family, or accompanied by a furry friend, being equipped for the journey makes all the difference in ensuring your trip is smooth, enjoyable, and memorable.

Before setting out, preparing your vehicle is essential. Begin by scheduling a comprehensive maintenance check-up. Ensuring your tires are in good condition, your brakes are functioning properly, and your fluids are topped off minimizes the chances of mechanical issues mid-trip. It's also a good idea to stock up on essentials for unexpected situations, such as a fully charged portable jump starter, a spare tire, and a tire repair kit. On a personal road trip through the Mojave Desert, my car's battery unexpectedly died at a remote rest stop. Thankfully, my portable jump starter saved the day, allowing me to continue my journey without waiting hours for assistance. Always keep your gas tank above half full, especially in rural or remote areas, to avoid being stranded far from the nearest gas station.

Mapping out your route is equally important. While modern navigation apps provide real-time directions and updates, having a physical map as a backup can be a lifesaver in areas with poor cell reception. On a trip through the Appalachian Mountains, I relied on an old-fashioned map when my GPS signal disappeared for hours, helping me find my way to the nearest town. A well-thought-out route includes planned stops for food, fuel, and rest while leaving room for spontaneity. Unplanned detours, like visiting a roadside museum or pulling over to take in a scenic overlook, often become the highlights of a road trip.

Emergencies can arise at any time, and staying calm is key to resolving them effectively. If you encounter car trouble, such as a breakdown, safely pull off the road, turn on your hazard lights, and assess the situation. Having an emergency roadside assistance plan, like one offered by your insurance company or AAA, can provide peace of mind and quick help when needed. For medical emergencies, knowing the location of nearby urgent care facilities or hospitals along your route is invaluable. Download apps like First Aid by the American Red Cross to guide you through basic medical procedures while waiting for professional assistance.

In today's digital age, technology enhances the road trip experience in countless ways. Apps such as Google Maps, Waze, and Roadtrippers help you plan routes, avoid traffic, and discover hidden gems along the way. For accommodations, apps like HotelTonight can secure last-minute lodging, while Yelp offers trusted reviews for local restaurants and attractions. During one trip across the Midwest, I discovered a charming roadside diner through an app recommendation—it turned out to be a family-run gem serving the best homemade pies I've ever tasted. Keeping a portable power bank or car charger handy ensures your devices remain functional throughout the journey.

Traveling with children requires an extra layer of planning to keep them entertained and comfortable. Audiobooks, educational games, and activity kits tailored to their age groups can make long stretches on the road more manageable. Scheduling regular breaks for snacks, bathroom stops, and some light exercise helps prevent restlessness. Involving children in the trip's planning can also make them feel engaged and excited. On one family road trip, I let my kids choose a roadside attraction from a list I'd prepared, and their excitement to see the "World's Largest Ball of Twine" turned out to be a highlight of the trip.

For pet owners, ensuring your furry companion is comfortable and safe during the journey is crucial. Start by packing all their essentials, including food, water, a leash, waste bags, and any medications they may need. If your pet isn't accustomed to long car rides, take them on shorter drives beforehand to acclimate them. A pet carrier or seat belt harness ensures their safety while you're driving. Research pet-friendly accommodations, parks, and attractions along your route to include your pet in the adventure. During one trip to the Pacific Northwest, my dog loved exploring dog-friendly hiking trails, which became a shared adventure I'll never forget.

Personal experiences often reveal the value of preparedness. During a journey through the Southwest, I encountered a sudden sandstorm that forced me to pull over. The experience reinforced the importance of always carrying plenty of water, as waiting for the storm to pass left me parched in the desert heat. Another time, a spur-of-the-moment decision to follow a road sign advertising a lavender farm led to a peaceful afternoon wandering fragrant fields, a reminder of the joys of embracing the unexpected.

Practical tips can help make the most of your trip. Packing a cooler with snacks and drinks reduces the need for frequent stops and saves money. Comfortable clothing, layers, and sturdy shoes are essential, especially if your route includes changing climates or impromptu hikes. Organizing your car so that frequently used items, such as chargers, maps, and toiletries, are within easy reach reduces stress during the journey. For nighttime driving, ensure your headlights and windshield are clean to maximize visibility, and plan rest breaks to avoid fatigue.

Safety should always be a priority on the road. Be mindful of your surroundings, especially when stopping in unfamiliar areas. Lock your doors and avoid leaving valuables in plain sight when parked. Share your travel plans with friends or family, including your estimated arrival times and key stops, so someone knows your whereabouts.

A road trip is as much about the journey as it is about the destination. With thoughtful preparation, a willingness to adapt, and a sense of adventure, you'll create an experience filled with memories that last a lifetime. From breathtaking landscapes to unexpected roadside discoveries, every mile traveled contributes to your unique travel story, offering a deeper connection to the world around you and a renewed appreciation for the freedom of the open road.

CHAPTER 19

When preparing for a trip, especially on a budget, the first priority is learning how to maximize value without sacrificing the experience. Start by planning your route carefully, focusing on fuel-efficient pathways. Opt for highways and routes that avoid excessive stops or heavy congestion. Apps designed to track fuel prices can be invaluable, allowing you to identify gas stations with the best rates along your journey. If you're venturing into remote areas, make sure to refuel in towns with affordable gas prices beforehand, as rural regions often have higher costs.

Finding economical lodging doesn't mean settling for a subpar experience. Online platforms often provide access to last-minute deals for hotels, motels, or short-term rentals. Hostels, known for their affordability, also create opportunities to meet like-minded travelers, fostering a sense of camaraderie. For those seeking more unique accommodations, consider staying with locals through homestay platforms. These arrangements not only save money but also offer a glimpse into the daily lives of the community. If you enjoy nature and adventure, campgrounds provide an excellent alternative, many of which are situated in picturesque locations that amplify the charm of your trip.

Food expenses, another significant aspect of travel budgets, can be controlled with thoughtful planning. Pack a variety of shelf-stable snacks before you hit the road. Local farmers' markets often offer fresh, affordable produce that reflects the region's flavors. Using these ingredients, you can create simple yet memorable meals, whether enjoying a picnic by a tranquil lake or at a bustling park. If dining out, skip tourist hotspots in favor of restaurants favored by locals. These establishments typically offer authentic cuisine at reasonable prices, often accompanied by a friendly, welcoming atmosphere.

Exploring a destination doesn't have to involve pricey activities. Many cities feature complimentary walking tours led by knowledgeable guides who share intriguing historical anecdotes and cultural tidbits. Museums frequently offer free admission days or reduced fees, especially for families or specific groups. Public parks, beaches, and nature reserves present opportunities to unwind and connect with the beauty of the surroundings at no cost. Time your visit to coincide with community events or festivals, as these occasions often highlight the local culture and provide entertainment free of charge.

Understanding available discounts can also stretch your travel budget. Attractions, transportation services, and even certain restaurants often provide special rates for seniors, military veterans, and students. Carrying proof of eligibility, such as an ID card, ensures you can take full advantage of these savings. Researching these benefits in advance equips you to make informed decisions throughout your trip.

Immersing yourself in the local culture is the essence of travel. Take the time to engage with residents—whether it's chatting with a shopkeeper, conversing with a street performer, or seeking advice from a café owner. Their insights often reveal hidden gems that are absent from guidebooks. On one occasion, I visited a small coastal town and struck up a conversation with a local fisherman. Not only did he share stories about his life at sea, but he also recommended a secluded beach that turned out to be the highlight of my trip.

Navigating unfamiliar places becomes easier when you approach the task systematically. Begin by familiarizing yourself with the area's layout through a map, either digital or paper-based. Use public transportation wherever possible, as it's both economical and environmentally friendly. Before you travel, download transit schedules and understand the fare system to ensure a smooth experience.

As you explore, let your curiosity guide you. Imagine wandering through cobblestone streets lined with colorful murals, each painting a unique story of the community's past and present. As you continue, the aroma of freshly brewed coffee might draw you to a quaint café, or you may hear the sound of a busker playing a familiar tune, adding a layer of charm to your adventure. Every corner has the potential to surprise and delight, making the experience all the more personal and memorable.

No app or book can replace the richness of firsthand experiences. Over the years, I've discovered that fully engaging with the culture, food, and traditions of a place transforms a trip into something far more meaningful. I still recall the morning I joined a local farmer to pick fresh strawberries in a sunlit field—a simple act that left me with a lasting appreciation for the region's agricultural heritage.

Preparing for unexpected situations is another essential part of travel planning. Bring along a basic first-aid kit, and familiarize yourself with the locations of nearby medical facilities. Know the local emergency contact numbers and keep digital and physical copies of your ID and passport in separate locations to safeguard against potential losses.

When you return home after a well-planned journey, the true value lies not in the number of landmarks you visited but in the connections you made, the cultures you experienced, and the memories that stay with you long after the trip has ended. Travel is not just about movement; it's about transformation, learning, and expanding your horizons in ways you never imagined.

CHAPTER 20

Traveling across the United States opens the door to an incredibly diverse and vibrant collection of experiences, ranging from metropolitan hubs buzzing with life to tranquil natural escapes that rejuvenate the soul. Before setting out on this adventure, it is important to familiarize yourself with the rules, customs, and nuances that shape travel in this vast country. Each state operates under its own unique laws and cultural norms, which can sometimes surprise visitors who are not accustomed to these variations. Starting with a solid foundation of knowledge ensures that your journey will be not only memorable but also hassle-free.

One of the most essential aspects of travel in the United States is understanding state-specific driving laws. Every state governs its roads differently, and these differences extend beyond just speed limits or road signs. For instance, some states like New York enforce strict penalties for using a mobile phone while driving, while others, such as Montana, may have more relaxed rules regarding open containers of alcohol in vehicles. It's always a wise idea to research and review the driving requirements of the states you'll be passing through. Keeping your driver's license, insurance documents, and vehicle registration on hand is mandatory and often checked during routine traffic stops. If you plan to rent a vehicle, ask the rental agency about interstate travel restrictions, as not all agreements permit crossing state borders. These precautions ensure you are prepared to handle any situation on the road with confidence.

America's national and state parks offer breathtaking scenery and unparalleled opportunities for outdoor exploration, but they come with their own set of rules. Visitors should familiarize themselves with park regulations, which are often aimed at protecting fragile ecosystems. For example, in some regions, visitors are prohibited from feeding wildlife or removing natural items such as rocks or plants. In highly protected areas like Yosemite or Yellowstone, permits are often required for backcountry camping, and rangers strictly enforce these guidelines. Seasonal restrictions, such as fire bans during dry months, are also common. Respecting these rules is not only about avoiding fines but also about contributing to the preservation of these natural wonders for future generations. I recall one unforgettable experience at Glacier National Park, where a ranger shared how a seemingly harmless action—like tossing breadcrumbs for birds—can disrupt local ecosystems and create long-term consequences.

Safety is an overarching priority for any traveler, especially in a country as expansive as the United States, where distances between towns or services can be significant. In case of emergencies, dialing 911 is the fastest way to connect with police, fire, or medical services. Many travelers, particularly those venturing into rural areas, may benefit from downloading offline maps and storing the contact numbers for local emergency services. It is also useful to research the availability of urgent care centers and hospitals in the vicinity of your travel route. In addition to medical emergencies, non-urgent situations—like getting locked out of your car or losing your wallet—can often be resolved by calling local non-emergency hotlines. A memorable personal experience in New Orleans taught me the value of these resources when a local hotline helped recover a misplaced item I had left in a ride-share vehicle.

Navigating public transportation is another key skill that enhances the overall travel experience in many U.S. cities. While much of the country relies on personal vehicles, urban areas like Chicago, Boston, and Washington, D.C., offer extensive public transit systems. First-time visitors often find it helpful to invest in city-specific transit passes, which provide unlimited access to buses, subways, and trains for a fixed period. These passes not only save money but also eliminate the hassle of buying individual tickets. In cities like San Francisco, hopping on a historic cable car offers both a convenient way to get around and a nostalgic glimpse into the city's past. Travelers should also consider using mobile apps to check real-time schedules and plan efficient routes. A local once shared with me in Philadelphia that timing your travel to avoid rush hours can turn what might have been a stressful commute into a leisurely ride.

Interacting with locals can significantly enrich your journey, offering insights and connections that no guidebook can replicate. Participating in community activities, such as farmers' markets, cultural festivals, or public workshops, often leads to authentic experiences. For instance, a visit to a small-town festival in Vermont introduced me to the art of maple syrup tapping, a tradition deeply ingrained in the local culture. Similarly, a casual chat with a shop owner in Portland, Oregon, led to an impromptu recommendation for a hidden coffee shop, where I spent hours immersed in the city's vibrant atmosphere.

Packing wisely is an often-overlooked aspect of travel, yet it plays a crucial role in ensuring comfort and preparedness. The United States spans a range of climates, so travelers should tailor their packing to the regions they plan to visit. For example, lightweight clothing and sturdy footwear are ideal for hiking in the Grand Canyon, while layered outfits and thermal gear are essential for exploring the icy expanses of Alaska. One practical tip is to include a versatile backpack equipped with essentials like a first-aid kit, refillable water bottle, and portable charger. For those traveling in the winter months, anti-slip shoe grips and compact snow scrapers can be lifesavers, particularly in states prone to heavy snowfall.

Another highlight of traveling in the United States is discovering the picturesque landscapes and roadside attractions that dot the country. Scenic drives, such as the Blue Ridge Parkway in Virginia or the Overseas Highway in Florida, offer stunning views that captivate even seasoned travelers. These routes often feature well-maintained pullouts and picnic spots, allowing you to pause and soak in the surroundings. While major cities like Los Angeles or Miami may dominate travel itineraries, smaller towns and rural regions often provide a more intimate glimpse into American life. Visiting a family-owned diner in Nebraska or attending a local craft fair in Wyoming can leave lasting impressions that are impossible to replicate elsewhere.

Lastly, every traveler benefits from staying informed about local laws and safety protocols. Beyond just road regulations, it's important to respect laws related to alcohol consumption, noise ordinances, and even pet restrictions. In some states, carrying open containers of alcohol in public spaces is prohibited, while others may have strict curfews in residential neighborhoods. Similarly, pet owners traveling with their furry companions should research leash laws and pet-friendly accommodations in advance. Staying aware of these nuances helps foster positive interactions with locals and ensures a smoother journey.

-

CHAPTER 22

Embarking on a journey through the United States is an adventure that promises an unforgettable mix of landscapes, cultures, and experiences. Whether you're exploring vibrant cities, serene rural towns, or breathtaking natural wonders, careful planning can make your trip both enjoyable and seamless. For first-time travelers, having a clear and practical guide can eliminate much of the guesswork and anxiety, ensuring every moment of the trip is as smooth and memorable as possible.

Begin by identifying your destination and gathering resources. Each state has an official tourism office that serves as a treasure trove of information. These offices provide maps, brochures, and travel guides that often include hidden gems not commonly found online. For instance, during a trip to Arizona, I discovered a remote but stunning canyon through a tip from the state's tourism website—a destination that quickly became the highlight of my adventure. Most tourism offices also maintain physical visitor centers staffed with experts who can tailor recommendations to your preferences. Stopping by one of these centers can provide insights into lesser-known attractions, local events, and special promotions.

Equally important is preparing for unforeseen circumstances. Compile a list of essential contacts, including local emergency services, roadside assistance providers, and nearby hospitals. Services like AAA offer 24/7 support for breakdowns, which can be especially useful if you're traveling by car. During one road trip through the Rocky Mountains, I encountered an unexpected tire issue, and a quick call to roadside assistance ensured I was back on the road in no time. It's also wise to save the numbers for local tourism hotlines, as they often provide real-time updates on closures, weather conditions, and other travel advisories.

Technology plays a significant role in modern travel, offering convenience and reliability at your fingertips. Navigation apps can help you find the fastest or most scenic routes, while fuel price trackers like GasBuddy save money on gas. Weather apps keep you informed about conditions that could affect your plans, ensuring you're prepared for sudden changes. During one summer trip to Florida, a weather app helped me avoid a thunderstorm by recommending alternate times for outdoor activities. Apps like Yelp and Google Maps are invaluable for finding restaurants, attractions, and reviews, but sometimes old-fashioned word-of-mouth recommendations from locals uncover the true gems of a destination.

Accommodations are another critical component of any trip. Whether you prefer hotels, motels, hostels, or unique stays like cabins or treehouses, platforms such as Airbnb and Booking.com provide extensive options to suit your budget and preferences. If you're traveling during a busy season, booking early ensures you secure the best deals and availability. On a visit to New York's Finger Lakes, I discovered a quaint lakeside cottage through a local lodging website, offering not just affordability but also a serene retreat away from the crowds.

Food is an integral part of experiencing any destination. To save on dining expenses, consider packing non-perishable snacks and researching markets where you can purchase fresh, local ingredients. Farmers' markets, in particular, offer a glimpse into the local culinary scene while supporting small vendors. Preparing a simple picnic can be both economical and delightful, allowing you to enjoy a meal in scenic spots like parks or along riverbanks. When dining out, prioritize eateries frequented by locals, as they often serve authentic and reasonably priced meals. During one trip to Louisiana, a small, family-owned restaurant recommended by a taxi driver turned out to offer the most flavorful gumbo I've ever tasted.

Exploring the United States doesn't have to come with a hefty price tag. Many cities offer free attractions, such as walking tours, public parks, and historic landmarks. Museums and cultural centers often have specific days with free or discounted entry, and local festivals provide entertainment, food, and music at little to no cost. On a visit to Chicago, I stumbled upon a free jazz festival in Millennium Park, which became a highlight of my trip, blending incredible music with a lively, welcoming atmosphere.

Interacting with locals enriches your journey and provides unique perspectives. A casual conversation with a shopkeeper, barista, or taxi driver can lead to valuable recommendations and insights into the region's culture. During a visit to Oregon, I struck up a conversation with a bookstore owner who directed me to a secluded coastal trail with views that felt like they belonged on a postcard. These personal connections often turn ordinary trips into extraordinary experiences.

Navigating an unfamiliar city can be daunting, but breaking it down into manageable steps simplifies the process. Begin with a map to understand the layout and key landmarks, then determine your transportation options. Public transit systems are often the most economical and efficient way to get around urban areas, and many cities offer passes that bundle unlimited rides for a set period. If walking is your preferred mode of exploration, invest in comfortable footwear and allow yourself to wander. Some of the best discoveries happen when you take a spontaneous turn down an unassuming street.

Preparation for unexpected situations ensures peace of mind. Carrying a small first-aid kit, along with copies of important documents like your ID and itinerary, can be invaluable. Keeping a portable charger for your phone and a backup power source for essential devices guarantees you stay connected. Having cash on hand in smaller denominations is also wise, especially for tipping or visiting places that don't accept cards.

Traveling is about more than just ticking landmarks off a list; it's about immersing yourself in the culture, history, and natural beauty of each place you visit. Whether you're watching the sunrise over the Grand Canyon, strolling through Savannah's cobblestone streets, or experiencing the energy of Times Square at night, every moment offers a chance to connect with something greater than yourself.

As you return home, the memories and stories you bring back will stay with you long after the journey ends. Each trip becomes a chapter in your life's story, shaping how you see the world and reminding you of the vastness and beauty it holds. Travel is not just a destination—it's a journey of discovery, connection, and transformation.

CHAPTER 23

Embarking on a journey across the United States is a thrilling opportunity to explore a land filled with diverse cultures, breathtaking landscapes, and countless hidden treasures. Whether you're navigating iconic cities, quaint small towns, or awe-inspiring natural landmarks, preparation and guidance can make all the difference in ensuring your trip is smooth, enjoyable, and filled with meaningful experiences. Picture yourself holding a guide that takes you step-by-step, like a seasoned traveler walking alongside you, explaining every detail with the clarity and simplicity of a trusted companion.

The first step in any successful journey begins with selecting your destination and understanding its geography. The United

States is vast, and each state offers unique experiences that cater to a wide range of interests. Imagine starting your adventure in California, a state where sun-drenched beaches, towering redwoods, and bustling cities coexist. If you're flying into Los Angeles, familiarize yourself with the city's layout. Use your travel map or app to pinpoint major landmarks like Hollywood Boulevard, the Getty Center, and Santa Monica Pier. Navigating a sprawling city like this might feel overwhelming at first, but breaking it into smaller sections—downtown, the beaches, and the Hollywood Hills—makes it far more manageable.

Once you've soaked in the vibrant energy of Los Angeles, your map might lead you along the Pacific Coast Highway, a route famed for its dramatic ocean views. The winding roads take you past picturesque stops like Malibu, Santa Barbara, and Big Sur, each offering its own charm. As you drive, pause at scenic overlooks to capture the beauty of the coastline. I recall one such stop where the sight of waves crashing against rocky cliffs left me awestruck, a memory etched in my mind long after the trip ended.

Continuing up the West Coast, your travels might bring you to Oregon, a state renowned for its lush greenery and artistic communities. Portland, known as the "City of Roses," serves as a hub for creativity and sustainability. Use your guide to navigate its vibrant neighborhoods, each offering something unique. From the food carts in downtown to the tranquil beauty of the Japanese Garden, the city is a blend of urban charm and natural splendor. Venture further into the state to discover the Columbia River Gorge, where waterfalls like Multnomah Falls cascade down moss-covered cliffs. The directions are straightforward, with well-marked trails that make this natural wonder accessible to visitors of all skill levels.

As your journey unfolds, the value of a reliable guide becomes even more evident.

Traveling through the Midwest, for instance, reveals a completely different side of the United States. The rolling prairies and farmland of Iowa and Kansas contrast sharply with the bustling metropolises of the coasts. In these areas, maps not only direct you to destinations but also help you uncover local gems that reflect the region's charm. During a visit to Nebraska, a local recommendation led me to a small diner serving the most incredible homemade pies. It's moments like these—unplanned and serendipitous—that often become the highlights of a trip.

Navigating large cities like Chicago or New York can be intimidating, but with a well-detailed map and practical tips, even first-time visitors can move through these urban jungles with ease. In Chicago, public transportation like the "L" train system is efficient and easy to understand once you've studied the map. Pair this with a walking guide that takes you along the Magnificent Mile, through Millennium Park, and up to the observation deck at Willis Tower for an unforgettable day in the Windy City.

Heading south, your guide might point you toward the rich cultural history of cities like Charleston, South Carolina, or New Orleans, Louisiana. These destinations are known for their vibrant architecture, unique cuisine, and deep historical roots. In Charleston, walking tours through the historic district reveal cobblestone streets, antebellum homes, and gardens that bloom year-round. New Orleans offers a sensory overload with its music, food, and colorful festivals. Use your map to navigate from the French Quarter to quieter neighborhoods like the Garden District, where oak-lined streets lead to quaint cafes and historic mansions.

No guide to the United States would be complete without exploring its natural wonders. Imagine standing at the edge of the Grand Canyon, looking out over a landscape that seems almost otherworldly in its vastness. Getting there is straightforward with a good map, which highlights the key entrances and viewpoints. The South Rim, accessible year-round, provides well-maintained trails and overlooks that are perfect for first-time visitors. If you're feeling adventurous, consider a mule ride down into the canyon or a helicopter tour for a bird's-eye view.

From the deserts of Arizona, your travels might take you north to Yellowstone National Park, a place of unparalleled geothermal activity and wildlife. Following clear signage and maps, you'll find geysers like Old Faithful erupting with clockwork precision, as well as serene hiking trails that lead to hidden waterfalls and open meadows. Traveling through the park feels like stepping into a nature documentary, with bison, elk, and even bears making appearances along the way.

Heading east, the Appalachian Mountains offer a completely different outdoor experience. Use your guide to plan stops along the Blue Ridge Parkway, a scenic drive that weaves through the mountains, offering breathtaking views and access to hiking trails. Small towns like Asheville, North Carolina, provide a perfect base for exploring the region's craft breweries, art galleries, and live music venues.

Throughout your journey, practical travel tips ensure you're always prepared. Keep a physical copy of your maps and travel plans, as technology isn't always reliable in remote areas. Pack essentials like a first-aid kit, snacks, and water, especially for long drives or hikes. Engage with locals whenever possible—they are often the best source of recommendations and can point you to places that aren't on the typical tourist radar. During one visit to Texas, a conversation with a park ranger led me to a hidden swimming hole that became a highlight of my trip.

As your journey concludes, you'll find that the maps and guides you relied on have become more than just tools for navigation—they are a record of your adventure. Each marked route and circled destination tells a story of discovery, connection, and wonder. The United States, with its incredible variety and endless opportunities for exploration, becomes more than a place—it becomes an experience, one that stays with you long after the journey ends.

Traveling is about more than just reaching a destination; it's about embracing the unknown, seeking out new perspectives, and creating memories that last a lifetime. With a detailed guide and a spirit of curiosity, every trip becomes a story worth telling.

Made in United States
Orlando, FL
13 December 2024